RAND NATIONAL DEFENSE RESEARCH INSTITUTE

Toward Resiliency in the Joint Blood Supply Chain

Brent Thomas, Katherine Anania, Anthony DeCicco, John A. Hamm

Prepared for the Defense Advanced Research Projects Agency

For more information on this publication, visit www.rand.org/t/RR2482

Library of Congress Cataloging-in-Publication Data is available for this publication.
ISBN: 978-1-9774-0137-3

Published by the RAND Corporation, Santa Monica, Calif.
© Copyright 2018 RAND Corporation
RAND® is a registered trademark.

Support RAND
Make a tax-deductible charitable contribution at
www.rand.org/giving/contribute

www.rand.org

Preface

The Joint military community provides a wide array of medical support services to its personnel. As in the civilian medical sphere, an essential component of that care is the provision of blood and blood products to patients, both in the United States and overseas. Blood is important not only for its use in a variety of medical therapies and treatments, but also for its utility to surgical patients and trauma victims. Ensuring that blood and blood products remain safe and available for patients requires sophisticated logistical support, especially for the military community's provision of blood to its medical operations around the globe.

However, some operating environments that the U.S. military might face in the future could lead to challenges in the operation of the blood supply chain, especially in sourcing, storage, and distribution. For example, peer and near-peer adversaries could conduct large-scale combat operations with a capability to significantly degrade the freedom of movement for U.S. forces. In those environments, combat action could result in significant demand spikes for blood while simultaneously limiting the capacity to transport products to forward operating locations. The Defense Advanced Research Project Agency's (DARPA's) Defense Sciences Office asked the RAND Corporation to examine these challenges and to explore mechanisms that might offer greater resiliency in the military's management of its blood supply chain operations.

This report is oriented toward a general readership interested in learning about blood supply chains, the challenges they may face, and mechanisms to strengthen them. Medical professionals with an interest in blood should also find the analysis of value, especially in its presentation of frameworks for exploring supply chain resiliency. Logisticians and supply chain managers for other product lines may find the examination of the blood supply chain useful as an analogue for exploring resiliency in their own operations.

This research was sponsored by DARPA and conducted within the Acquisition and Technology Policy Center of the RAND National Defense Research Institute, a federally funded research and development center sponsored by the Office of the Secretary of Defense, the Joint Staff, the Unified Combatant Commands, the Navy, the Marine Corps, the defense agencies, and the defense Intelligence Community.

For more information on the RAND Acquisition and Technology Policy Center, see www.rand.org/nsrd/ndri/centers/atp or contact the director (contact information is provided on the webpage).

Contents

Figures and Tables

Figures

Tables

Summary

The Joint military community provides a wide array of medical support services to its personnel. As in the civilian medical sphere, an essential component of that care is the provision of blood and blood products to its service members at home and abroad. Blood is an important element of medical supply, given its use in a variety of medical therapies and treatments. Furthermore, its use is critical and often life-saving in the treatment of surgical patients and trauma victims.

Blood requires sophisticated logistical protocols and materiel handling procedures to ensure that its use is safe for patients. From the point of collection from a donor to testing and processing in the lab, during transportation to and storage in medical treatment facilities, and on to eventual patient use, blood is carefully logged and tracked. Moreover, throughout the supply chain, blood must be handled and maintained at appropriate temperatures to ensure its safety for patients.

There are four products most commonly handled in blood supply chain operations: fresh whole blood and its three principal components, red blood cells, platelets, and plasma.[1]

- *Fresh whole blood* is provided by volunteer donors. However, the unit that a donor provides is generally not the product that would be transfused to a patient, except under some emergency circumstances. Once a unit of whole blood has been collected from a donor, it is tested in the laboratory to ensure its safety for subsequent transfusion. Tested whole blood units will next be separated into three constituent components, generally by being spun in a centrifuge.
- *Red blood cells* carry oxygen throughout the body. Patients who suffer from anemia or have lost blood due to a trauma injury could be likely candidates for a transfusion of red blood cells. For longer-term storage, red cells can be processed and subsequently frozen, where multiple steps are required to convert between the frozen and liquid states.

---

[1] With the exception of specifically referenced components, from this point forward, we will refer to blood and blood products more simply as *blood*.

- *Platelets* act as the body's primary agent in clotting when blood vessels are damaged. Once platelets have gathered around the site where damage has occurred, they effectively plug the hole to promote clotting action, thereby limiting blood loss. Patients who could benefit from platelets include those with abnormal platelet function or who have suffered severe hemorrhage in the wake of a major trauma injury.
- *Plasma* accounts for over half the volume of blood, acting as the fluid in which platelets and red blood cells are transported through the body. Plasma contains a variety of elements essential to healthy blood function, such as water, glucose, and a diverse array of proteins and clotting factors. Plasma is most useful for patients who may be actively bleeding or who otherwise suffer from clotting factor deficiencies.

The U.S. military manages blood through a global network of collection points, testing labs, processing centers, warehouses for both frozen and liquid blood, transshipment centers, overseas medical treatment facilities, and storage sites for use by forces at operating locations far forward. We next highlight a few of these in more detail.

- *Blood donation centers* serve as the backbone for military blood collection services. They are generally associated with a nearby brick-and-mortar military medical treatment facility, which offers facile access to a wide array of laboratory assets and personnel to aid in the processing and coordination of serological testing of donated blood.
- *Armed Services Whole Blood Processing Labs* act as the central points for receipt of blood shipments from donation centers in the United States and for processing that blood for air shipments to medical treatment facilities located around the globe. These two facilities are also equipped to process and to ship frozen blood.
- *Blood Product Depots* manage the long-term storage of frozen blood in theater. These depots effectively act as storage points for large volumes of frozen buffer stock. Their design is to absorb the initial brunt of demand shocks that may occur during combat operations, providing blood until the two processing labs can surge their operations and develop pipelines from the United States.
- *Expeditionary Blood Transshipment Centers* act as the central receiving and shipment points for blood within a theater of operations. Each transshipment center is a portable capability that would be established at a large forward aerial port of debarkation, receiving its stock from the processing labs and ultimately acting as a local distribution hub to provide blood to medical support operations farther forward.
- *Blood Support Detachments* can receive blood shipments from the transshipment centers and are equipped to store and re-ice them as needed. These support detachments can operate in conjunction with Blood Product Depots to receive

thawed blood as well. Furthermore, they can collect fresh whole blood to support emergency demands, such as the provision of blood for a surge in trauma patients after combat action.

One scenario that is viewed as especially stressing to the military's blood supply chain is the possibility of a large-scale conflict against an adversary capable of generating a contested, degraded, or operationally limited combat environment. Over the past few decades, the defense community has taken increasing note of potential adversaries across the globe who have focused significant research into the development of long-range, high-precision conventional missile capabilities. In the employment of these missile systems across a theater of operations, an adversary could significantly degrade the freedom of movement for U.S. forces by targeting critical military infrastructure, including command and control centers, runways, and fuel depots.

The widespread occurrence of blast events would also likely generate significant numbers of casualties, many incurring severe trauma injuries. Over the course of a protracted series of missile strikes, the resulting trauma casualties would yield a long-term, large-scale demand signal for blood. Furthermore, these same strikes would limit the timely movement of blood into the theater from donation centers and warehouses in the continental United States. As the conflict wears on, blood in local storage at medical treatment facilities across the theater could be depleted, leading to challenges in providing blood in sufficient quantity to combat casualties.

In light of the challenges that might eventuate in the military's future combat environments, the defense community has begun to explore alternative capabilities, technologies, and concepts of operation that might afford additional flexibility in military operations. To that end, the Defense Advanced Research Projects Agency stood up a program known as the Complex Adaptive System Composition and Design Environment (CASCADE). In this program, researchers are developing novel mathematical frameworks to explore approaches for augmenting operational resiliency.

For the analysis here, we examined potential challenges to the Joint blood supply chain through the lens of this program. While we do not address the specifics of any specific mathematical constructs in this report, we do focus on the integration of three resiliency principles central to the CASCADE effort—fractionation, composition, and functional substitution:

- *Fractionation* enables the scaling of elements within the supply chain to deploy capabilities relative to the level of their need farther downrange. It may be important to expedite the deployment of a small expeditionary capability to pave the way for follow-on augmentation capabilities. For example, a small blood collection center could be rapidly deployed and employed until a larger capability could be established with follow-on forces and supplies.

- *Composition* supports the tailoring of capabilities to best meet downrange needs. For example, a small Army medical brigade does not typically deploy with equipment to handle the thawing and processing of frozen blood. The Air Force, however, does have a small deployable capability that offers these services. Under some circumstances, it may prove useful to deploy the Air Force's team in concert with the Army brigade.
- *Functional substitution* looks for opportunities to amend currently used stocks and capabilities with substitutes better tailored to operational needs. For example, medical research and development could be targeted to provide approaches and technologies to replace current short-lived blood products with longer-lasting alternatives.

To enhance access to blood supplies and their delivery to medical treatment facilities at forward operating locations, a variety of approaches might be leveraged. Some practices may need to be revisited, such as Cold War–era airdrop of palletized blood. Other mechanisms are emerging technologies, such as stem cell–based production of red blood cells in laboratory bioreactors. While promising in their capacity for risk mitigation and distributed access to blood supplies, nascent technologies will require further research and development to improve their cost-effectiveness. Other methods may incur some risk in their implementation, such as the activation of walking blood banks to collect blood at remote operating locations, or the utilization of a partner nation's blood supplies. There may also be value in employing alternate delivery platforms, such as unmanned aerial vehicles. Existing technology here is sufficiently advanced that these assets can be designed or tailored for blood delivery requirements relative to operational parameters, such as payload, distance, and speed.

A portfolio of additional mitigation options offers promise for improving blood supply chain operations, starting from deployed medical facilities and spanning downrange during contingency operations to the point of injury. Some approaches employ lessons learned from decades prior, such as freeze-drying plasma and refrigerating platelets to extend their shelf lives. Other mitigations, such as using tranexamic acid to limit blood loss and employing tactical buddy transfusion to provide access to supply at the point of injury, offer recognized benefits but have not yet entered mainstream use, potentially requiring training to promote awareness and employment protocols. Still other techniques in the research and development pipeline may become available in the near- to mid-term, including technologies to accelerate frozen red cell thawing and processing and mechanisms to limit blood loss due to severe trauma injuries to the torso. Other evolving technologies may require significant time to reach broader application, such as synthetic oxygen carriers to substitute for traditional red blood cells and bioelectrical stimulation techniques to limit blood loss.

Furthermore, other classes of mitigation might also add resiliency to the Joint blood supply chain. For example, access to energy is key in keeping blood at the right temperatures, and the availability of communications plays an important role in ensuring timely resupply of blood. However, during contingencies such as natural disasters or large-scale combat, access to these resources may be degraded. This suggests the potential value in leveraging alternatives, such as redundancy in diesel generators and training to use low-bandwidth communication modes. Risks in activation of mitigation approaches might need to be managed, including using technologies such as pathogen inactivation to limit the risk of transfusion-related infection from partner nation blood supplies and the potential to recruit donors whose blood has especially low antigen levels as a mitigation against adverse transfusion reactions.

Overall, the intent of this research is to stimulate discussion in the Joint medical community to help in the exploration of where resiliency measures may be needed in the overall blood supply chain. By examining mechanisms for resiliency across the blood supply chain, this community can be better equipped to tailor a robust portfolio of resiliency investments. Such a portfolio would better ensure the availability and safety of blood under a wide array of system stressors and threat conditions.

Over the course of the analysis, several key themes emerged.

Systemwide modeling frameworks are essential to understanding supply chain operations. To frame a common basis for examining supply chain operations, it is critical to have a flexible, systemwide view. With a model that can account for and integrate a range of different supply chain operations, it is possible to assess resiliency measures that can support an individual medical treatment facility as well as those supporting a theaterwide network of medical treatment facilities.

Understand stressors that may challenge the supply chain. Whether undertaking an assessment of historical experiences of mass casualty events or participating in a table-top exercise to explore possible future combat operations, a community of practitioners can posit scenarios both reasonable and extreme. When those stressors are applied in concert with a supply chain modeling framework, their outcomes can then be examined to determine effects on the supply chain. The outcome of these stress tests will highlight supply chain processes in need of attention.

Identify gaps or brittleness in current capabilities. Understanding simply that an element is brittle is insufficient—knowing how it became a gap and identifying the circumstances under which it will fail are essential. For example, a supply stockout at a treatment facility forward might drive consideration for augmented storage there. However, if that stockout was more a failure of transportation to provide sufficient throughput of blood, an extra refrigerator will ultimately prove inadequate. With nuanced information in hand, it then becomes possible to think through the mitigation approaches appropriate to bridge the capability gap.

Explore how current capabilities, evolving technologies, and alternative concepts of operation can mitigate those gaps. Here, understanding the "why" from the previous point is most useful. For example, is there a functional substitute for the blood that stocked out in the stress test? Is it possible to cost-effectively procure more testing or collection equipment that proved to be shortfalls? Could the limited capabilities of a forward operating unit be augmented by a small, agile capability from another service? A multidisciplinary and multiservice approach can help to better expose capabilities outside the scope of individual communities, especially in exploring the tripartite resiliency dimensions of functional substitution, alternative composition, and fractionation of capability.

Ensure that mitigations function on the scales needed. Some resiliency options, such as accelerating the capability to thaw and process frozen blood, can offer significant throughput capability for a short time to a local catchment area. However, if a broader network of treatment facilities requires longer-term support, leveraging options such as partner nation blood support may be warranted.

Combined mitigations can offer strengths that individual solutions may not. Here, it is essential to think through the broader dimensions of resiliency to determine where options may need to be linked. For example, partner nation blood support can be coupled with pathogen inactivation capabilities to ensure access to safer supplies. Similarly, combining the prophylactic use of tranexamic acid for forces on high-risk combat missions with reliable resupply of blood and medical supplies by unmanned aerial vehicle offers opportunities for longer-term support than either mitigation alone.

Ultimately, going through this process of supply chain stress assessment will yield a better roadmap toward enhanced resiliency in blood operations. With adherence to that roadmap, the military's medical support network will be better prepared to provide quality care to its patients under a wider array of system stressors, contingency considerations, and threat conditions.

Acknowledgments

The military's blood community is small but exceptionally passionate in its dedication to medical support. Our work would have truly been impossible without its backing and encouragement. All names and ranks shown here reflect the positions held as of the time the team engaged with them. Although many people contributed to this effort, the responsibility for the content of the analysis here lies with the authors.

First, we thank our sponsor and the team of researchers supporting the Complex Adaptive System Composition and Design Environment. John Paschkewitz and Sean Winkler were instrumental in guiding the team at the RAND Corporation toward a deeper exploration of sensitivities within the Joint blood supply chain.

We received tremendous support from the Air Force medical community. Lt Gen Mark Ediger, Maj Gen Dorothy Hogg, Maj Gen Roosevelt Allen, Brig Gen Bob Miller, Col Matt Hanson, and Lt Col Julie Skinner were pivotal in helping us integrate critical blood equities.

The Armed Service Blood Program and its service program offices also generously shared their expertise. COL Audra Taylor, CDR Suyen Teran, LTC Jason Corley, Lt Col Kathryn Shaw, Lt Col Jessica Hughes, Lt Col Angela Hudson, and Maj Sherry Glenn shared numerous insights.

The military's medical research community was equally crucial in its support, especially through the Joint Trauma System, the Army Institute for Surgical Research, and researchers in the American Association of Blood Banks network. We would like to extend our heartfelt thanks to COL Andre Cap, Col Stacy Shackelford, and Dustin Kinzinger for their insights.

The global combatant commands and their service blood program leads were central to the work. Insights from LCDR Steven Clifford, LCDR Wil Morales, LCDR Frederick Matheu, and MAJ Chris Evans helped to shape our understanding of blood planning around the globe.

The team at Travis Air Force Base was pivotal to our understanding of the wide array of services the Armed Services Whole Blood Processing Labs offer. 1st Lt Rafael Dy, HM1 Alphonso Johnson, Rhonda Rooney, Michael Butac, and the rest of the team graciously shared their time and expertise.

Operations support leads at military medical treatment facilities around the world also shared their insights on the role of blood support at the local level. Especially crucial to the foundations of the analysis were Col Peter Breed, Col Michelle Aaron, Col Brian Casleton, Lt Col Robert Peltzer, LTC Molly Sloan, Maj Nicole Ferguson, and MSgt Chad Below.

The Special Operations community was invaluable in shaping the team's understanding of blood support in the far forward. We are especially grateful for the insights shared by COL Sean Keenan, Col Rudy Cachuela, Col Paul Martin, LTC Ethan Miles, and Lt Col Becky Carter.

Finally, the team extends its warmest thanks to our fellow RAND colleagues, particularly Cynthia Cook, Chris Mouton, Ed Chan, Andrew Mulcahy, Ritika Chaturvedi, Sarah Nowak, and Brad DeBlois. The team is indebted to them for their support and insights throughout the analysis.

Abbreviations

A2/AD	anti-access/area denial
AABB	formerly known as American Association of Blood Banks
AFBPO	Air Force Blood Program Office
ASBP	Armed Services Blood Program
ASWBPL	Armed Services Whole Blood Processing Lab
BDC	blood donation center
BPD	Blood Product Depot
BSD	Blood Support Detachment
C3	command, control, and communications
CASCADE	Complex Adaptive System Composition and Design Environment
CDO	contested, degraded, or operationally limited
DARPA	Defense Advanced Research Projects Agency
EBSC	Expeditionary Blood Support Center
EBTC	Expeditionary Blood Transshipment Center
FBPT	Frozen Blood Product Team
FDA	U.S. Food and Drug Administration
FDP	freeze-dried plasma
FFP	fresh frozen plasma
FRBC	frozen red blood cells
FWB	fresh whole blood
HBOC	hemoglobin-based oxygen carrier
HBV	hepatitis B virus

HCV	hepatitis C virus
HIV	human immunodeficiency virus
HTLV	human T-cell lymphotropic virus
ICARUS	Inbound, Controlled, Air-Releasable, Unrecoverable Systems
LAPE	low-altitude parachute extraction
LTOWB	low-titer O whole blood
mL	milliliter
MTF	military treatment facility
PRBC	packed red blood cells
PROPPR	Pragmatic Randomized Optimal Platelet and Plasma Ratio
RBC	red blood cell
REBOA	resuscitative endovascular balloon occlusion of the aorta
SOF	Special Operations Forces
TACAD	tactical air delivery
TXA	tranexamic acid
UAV	unmanned aerial vehicle
WBB	walking blood bank
WSS	wound stasis system

CHAPTER ONE

An Introduction to the Joint Blood Supply Chain

The Joint military community provides a wide array of medical support services to its personnel. As in the civilian medical sphere, an essential component of that care is the provision of blood and blood products to its service members at home and abroad. Blood is an important element of medical supply, given its use in a variety of medical therapies and treatments. Moreover, its use is critical and often life-saving in the treatment of surgical patients and trauma victims.

Blood requires a sophisticated range of logistical protocols and materiel handling procedures to ensure that its use is safe for patients. From the point of collection with a donor to testing and processing in the lab, during transportation to and storage in medical treatment facilities, and onward to eventual transfusion into a patient, blood is carefully logged and tracked. Moreover, throughout its residence in the supply chain, blood must be handled and maintained at appropriate temperatures to ensure its safe use.

Given the global scope and extent of the provision of care in the Joint community, the efficient and effective management of the military's blood supply chain requires careful planning. The Armed Services Blood Program (ASBP) oversees the management and administration of blood in the military supply chain and recognizes the centrality of these factors.[1] In fact, the ASBP's credo offers its commitment to provide blood "to the right place at the right time in the right amount at the right temperature."[2]

Blood and Blood Products

To set the stage for exploring blood support for military operations, it will first be important to provide a fundamental understanding of the essential commodities man-

---

[1]   While it was established as a joint field operating agency over 60 years ago, the Defense Health Agency brought the ASBP under the aegis of its J3 operations directorate in 2017.

[2]   Carla Voorhees, "Armed Services Blood Program Supports Patient Care Worldwide," press release, U.S. Department of Defense, January 24, 2012.

aged by the Joint blood supply chain enterprise. Next, we will define the most commonly encountered blood products managed in the military medical system, outlining their function, their use in transfusion, and basic procedures for their handling.[3]

Fresh Whole Blood

Blood first enters the supply chain after being provided by a volunteer donor. Donors are initially screened to determine whether they have risk characteristics for the transmission of pathogens, such as hepatitis B or C virus (HBV or HCV). This careful screening offers an important mechanism to help mitigate against the risk of passing pathogens to a recipient through transfusion. A donor is generally allowed to provide only one unit of fresh whole blood (FWB) every 56 days. This allows the donor's body time to recover, providing a safe window to produce another unit of blood.

Under some emergency circumstances that we will later outline, FWB can be transfused. If it is, FWB must be transfused within 24 hours of collection when stored at room temperature and typically within 21 days if refrigerated, once treated with a preservative agent.[4] Adherence to these time lines mitigates against the risk of bacterial growth in the donated blood and limits the degree to which its potency may degrade.

However, the unit that a donor provides is generally not the blood that would be transfused to a patient. Once a unit of FWB has been collected (typically a volume of about 450 milliliters [mL]), that unit is tested in the laboratory to ensure its safety for subsequent transfusion. The lab will run a panel of assays and screening tests to evaluate the presence of a number of disease vectors, such as human immunodeficiency virus (HIV) and human T-cell lymphotropic virus (HTLV).[5] Should any pathogens be detected, the blood will be removed from the supply chain and securely destroyed.

After testing, FWB will be separated into its constituent components—red cells, platelets, and plasma. Current medical best practices favor the use of these individual components over the use of FWB in treating patients, as the care for each patient can be better tailored through the selection of blood products suited to that patient's condition. By customizing these portfolios of individual blood products, a medical provider can also mitigate against the potential for an adverse reaction during transfusion, such

---

[3] With the exception of specifically referenced components, from this point forward, we will refer to blood and blood products more simply as *blood*.

[4] The refrigerated shelf-life for FWB is a function of the choice in preservative agent added to the product. The American Red Cross offers a succinct outline of basic blood storage characteristics on its website (American Red Cross, "Blood Components," online fact sheet, 2018).

[5] The ASBP follows the screening protocols developed by the U.S. Food and Drug Administration (FDA). Given their application in medical therapies, blood falls under FDA's regulatory authority to protect both the donor and the recipient. FDA protocols include screening for a range of other factors, including West Nile virus, Zika virus, and the pathogens responsible for syphilis and Chagas disease. Readers can refer to the FDA website (fda.gov) for more information.

as hemolysis. The properties of these three individual component products are outlined next.

Packed Red Blood Cells

Red cells in blood carry oxygen throughout the body. Patients who suffer from anemia or have lost blood due to a trauma injury could be likely candidates for a transfusion of red blood cells. To obtain this product, a unit of FWB can be spun in a centrifuge, allowing for the separation of one unit of packed red blood cells (PRBC). A unit of PRBC may also receive further processing to filter out or to irradiate white blood cells, yielding a product referred to as a *leukoreduced unit of red cells*. Leukoreduced products can be especially beneficial to a patient whose immune system is compromised.

In addition to centrifugation of FWB, PRBC can also be obtained directly from a donor through a process known as apheresis collection. During apheresis, the donor is connected to a device that draws whole blood. The apheresis unit separates red cells from the blood via centrifugation as blood is collected from the donor, returning the non-PRBC blood components back into the donor. Depending on the apheresis device, the separation of PRBCs may occur in a continuous flow process (which requires two venipunctures in the donor) or in a more intermittent fashion (which uses only a single venipuncture). Through the ability of apheresis to return non-targeted blood products back to the donor, a patient may donate twice the count of red blood cells relative to more traditional donation methods.

Once produced, a unit of PRBC will also receive a small allotment of a preservative solution, such as citrate phosphate dextrose adenine (CPDA-1). Depending on the choice of preservative, PRBC, when refrigerated between 1 and 6 degrees Celsius, will have a shelf-life upward of 42 days. With appropriate containerization and packing materials, PRBC can be kept cold and shipped around the world to forward locations where military units may be postured. The sustainment of protocols to ensure that containers of PRBC do not fall out of the targeted temperature range is known as cold chain management.[6] This is a central feature in the management of blood, yielding handling challenges found in only a small range of products in other military supply chains.

While not as common in civilian application as in military environments, PRBC can also be further processed and frozen. First noted in the 1950s, targeted addition of compounds like glycerol can prevent water from entering, expanding, and rupturing the red cell body during the freezing of PRBC.[7] In current procedures, a unit of PRBC

---

[6]   Where power is used, such as in the employment of refrigerators, handling protocols are more specifically referred to as active cold chain management. Where electricity does not play a role, such as in the packing of coolers with blood and ice, this is known as passive management of the cold chain.

[7]   For more on the origins of FRBC processing, readers can refer to A. U. Smith, "Prevention of Haemolysis During Freezing and Thawing of Red Blood Cells," *The Lancet*, Vol. 2, December 30, 1950, p. 910.

receives a carefully controlled dosing of a cryoprotective agent, such as glycerol, using a specialized cell processor.

The resulting product is referred to as a unit of frozen red blood cells (FRBC), which needs to be stored in specialized freezer units at a temperature no greater than –65 degrees Celsius. Relative to a unit of PRBC, the additional equipment needed to produce and store FRBC ultimately adds cost to their production. However, the ability to freeze red cells significantly augments their longevity—FRBC have a shelf-life of ten years, roughly two orders of magnitude longer than PRBC.

Before FRBC can be transfused into a patient, the frozen unit must first be thawed. Once the blood has returned to a liquid state, the unit must then re-run through the specialized cell processor to extract the cryoprotective agent. Once thawed and deglycerolized, the red cells can be refrigerated and stored for up to 14 days before use.[8]

Platelets

Another important component of FWB, platelets act as the primary agent in clotting when blood vessels are damaged. Once platelets have gathered around the site where damage has occurred, they begin to change their shape, activating to effectively plug the hole, thereby promoting clotting action and preventing blood loss from the vessel. Patients who could benefit from platelets include those with abnormal platelet function (such as individuals suffering from thrombocytopenia) or patients who have a low platelet count (as can occur after severe blood loss in the wake of a major trauma injury).

Much as in the production of PRBC, platelets can be manufactured either through the centrifugation of FWB or from apheresis collection. Once collected, platelets can be stored at room temperature (between 20 and 24 degrees Celsius), where they have a shelf-life of five days.[9] Beyond this five-day window, platelets run an increasing risk of bacterial contamination, and their function will rapidly decline (a phenomenon known as *platelet storage lesion*). It is important to note that, during this period, platelets have a natural inclination to clot if they are not in motion. Consequently, they are typically stored on a specialized rack system called a *shake table* that gently agitates the platelets and prevents the clotting behavior.

---

[8]   Holley and his coauthors offer useful insights on the value of frozen blood products, especially in austere environments (A. Holley, D. C. Marks, L. Johnson, M. C. Reade, J. F. Badloe, and F. Noorman, "Frozen Blood Products: Clinically Effective and Potentially Ideal for Remote Australia," *Anaesthesia and Intensive Care*, Vol. 41, No. 1, January 2013, pp. 10–19, .

[9]   It is important to note that this abbreviated shelf-life relative to other blood products limits the ability to ship platelets to more distant forward operating locations.

Plasma

Plasma is the final principal component of FWB. Plasma accounts for over half the volume of blood, acting as the fluid in which platelets and red blood cells are transported through the body. Plasma contains a variety of elements essential to healthy blood function, such as water and glucose, as well as a diverse array of proteins and clotting factors. Plasma is most useful for patients who may be actively bleeding or who otherwise suffer from clotting factor deficiencies.[10]

As with the other blood components discussed so far, plasma can be produced either from the centrifugation of FWB or from apheresis. Unlike red blood cells (RBCs), plasma does not require an intensive process for its freezing and thawing, so it is typically stored frozen as a mechanism for enhancing its shelf-life. If frozen soon after collection, it is designated as fresh frozen plasma (FFP), and if frozen slightly later, it is labeled as PF24 (plasma frozen within 24 hours of phlebotomy). Frozen plasma is stored at temperatures no warmer than −18 degrees Celsius, a temperature notably higher than the requirements for FRBC. Frozen plasma can be stored for up to one year before use.

Other Blood Products

Plasma also serves as the source for a range of other specialty blood products. Depending on the fraction of interest, they can be extracted either from freshly drawn plasma or processed from FFP. Many of these products are derived from the wide array of clotting factors in plasma, which are typically identified using a nomenclature of Roman numerals (e.g., factor VII, factor IX). Many of these concentrated plasma extracts can be used to improve function in patients with low clotting-factor levels. Another common plasma derivative is cryoprecipitate (more commonly referred to simply as "cryo"), which comprises a mixture of plasma-clotting factors. Cryoprecipitate can be useful in a variety of scenarios, including in the treatment of hemophiliac patients and casualties suffering from massive hemorrhage.

Except for platelets, blood products tend to have shelf-lives ranging from weeks to years and require careful cold-chain management to ensure their safe use. While we have provided only a fundamental primer here on the production, use, and management of blood, there is a considerable body of detailed literature related to modern transfusion medicine and its practice. More comprehensive references, such as those by

---

[10]   In a set of recent medical trials, some U.S. cities have begun carrying plasma in ambulances for immediate treatment of trauma patients (Mark Holmberg, "Richmond Ambulances to Carry Plasma—A First for the Nation," WTVR News, 2014; P. S. Reynolds, M. J. Michael, E. D. Cochran, J. A. Wegelin, and B. D. Spiess, "Prehospital Use of Plasma in Traumatic Hemorrhage [the PUPTH Trial]: Study Protocol for a Randomized Controlled Trial," *Trials*, Vol. 16, p. 321, 2015). The trial study was conducted in Pittsburgh, Pennsylvania; Richmond, Virginia; and Denver, Colorado.

Harmening (2012) and Flynn (1998),[11] offer greater depth on issues related to blood, including details on biochemistry, molecular biology, genetics, and pathology.

Elements in the Joint Blood Supply Chain

With this introductory foundation in blood, we will next outline the basic building blocks in the military's blood supply chain. The U.S. military operates a network of collection, testing, transportation, and storage functions. This includes a number of fixed facilities within the United States and several military installations abroad, as well as some specialized supply chain operations that can deploy in support of down-range military operations. This network enables the military to support its domestic patient base as well as service members deployed to remote locations abroad. While the discussion that follows will not touch on detailed logistics processes, such as blood demand projection, donor recruitment, resupply ordering, or maintenance of laboratory equipment, it should orient readers to the fundamental operational nodes within the military's blood supply chain.

Blood Donation Centers

The source of the blood supply chain begins with its donor population, and the military's blood donation centers (BDCs) serve as the backbone for collection services. There is a total of 20 BDCs worldwide, and 16 are situated in the continental United States. The Army operates ten of the BDCs, whereas the Navy runs seven and the Air Force manages three.[12] BDCs provide a range of services, from scheduling blood drives, screening donors, collecting and testing blood, producing individual products such as PRBC, FFP, and cryo, to shipping blood to other facilities. BDCs are generally associated with a brick-and-mortar military medical treatment facility (MTF). With a nearby MTF, the BDC has more facile access to a wide array of laboratory assets and personnel to aid in the processing and coordination of serological testing of donated blood. Together, the centers collect approximately 150,000 units of blood each year from donors.[13] Each BDC is postured to provide blood both for MTFs in its vicinity and for eventually routing to support MTFs abroad.[14]

---

[11] Denise M. Harmening, *Modern Blood Banking and Transfusion Practices*, Philadelphia, Pa.: F.A. Davis Company, 2012; John C. Flynn, Jr,. *Essentials of Immunohematology*, Philadelphia, Pa.: W. B. Saunders Company, 1998.

[12] For more on the distribution of BDCs, readers can consult the ASBP website, including ASBP, "Where to Give Blood," online fact sheet, undated.

[13] U.S. Pacific Command, J07 Directorate, "USPACOM Blood Update," Honolulu, Hawaii, 2015.

[14] For more-detailed information on the tactical doctrine underpinning BDCs and many other elements in the blood supply chain, refer to U.S. Air Force, "Blood Support Operations," Air Force Tactics, Techniques, and Procedures 3-42.711, 2013.

Armed Services Whole Blood Processing Labs

For blood that is designated for shipment overseas rather than for use at a local MTF, its next destination is one of the military's two Armed Services Whole Blood Processing Labs (ASWBPLs). These facilities act as the central points for receipt of blood shipments from BDCs and for processing the blood for air shipments to MTFs located around the globe. The U.S. military currently operates two ASWBPLs, one on the east coast at Joint Base McGuire-Dix-Lakehurst in New Jersey (designated as ASWBPL-East), while the West Coast location is at Travis Air Force Base, California (also called ASWBPL-West). In addition to handling storage, shipment, and processing of liquid products, the ASWBPLs are equipped to ship frozen products such as FFP and FRBC for their long-term storage within the military's various regional areas of responsibility across the globe.

ASWBPL-East was the first of the two facilities, opening in 1955 after the Korean War. It played its first major role in support of combat operations during the Vietnam conflict. At that time, its mission was especially crucial, as preservative agents used in PRBC at the time allowed for only a 21-day shelf-life. This emphasized the need for efficient processing and shipment of blood to support combat operations forward. ASWBPL-West opened in 1995 to provide dedicated blood support to the Pacific theater, while its eastern counterpart shifted its focus to provide more dedicated support to Europe and the Middle East.

The ASWBPLs are under the operational control of the Air Force Blood Program Office (AFBPO), but they are each staffed jointly, with three personnel from each service.[15] The ASWBPLs have the capability to glycerolize and freeze (as well as deglycerolize and thaw) red blood cells. They can store and process up to 1,000 units of liquid RBCs, 1,000 units of frozen plasma, and 500 units of FRBC per week. The ASWBPLs are also capable of storing an additional 1,000 units of frozen plasma and 2,000 units of FRBC as a reserve stock for use in contingency support. With this mixture of functions, the ASWBPLs can be thought of as large, multicommodity warehouses that act as distribution hubs in support of global military operations.

Blood Product Depots

While the ASWBPLs can be viewed as blood depots within the continental United States, the warehousing function downrange in key areas of military operations is managed at Blood Product Depots (BPDs). BPDs are currently operated around the globe in Japan, Korea, Italy, and Afghanistan. The primary function of the BPDs is to manage the long-term storage of frozen blood in theater, where each BPD has the capability not only to store, but also to thaw and deglycerolize FRBC. In this fashion, the

---

[15] The Army and the Navy each have their own service-specific Blood Program Offices as well. Given the utility in locating the ASWBPLs at primary Air Force aerial ports of embarkation, operational control of the ASWBPLs falls to the AFBPO. However, given the doctrinal consideration that blood is a jointly managed resource, the ASWBPLs operate with this distinctly Joint service representation in their staffing.

BPDs effectively act as storage points for large volumes of frozen buffer stock. Their design is to absorb the initial brunt of demand shocks that may occur during military contingency operations, providing blood until ASWBPLs can surge operations and develop pipelines from the United States. The BPDs are each operated by individual components, but they provide blood for use by all the services. The storage and deglycerolization throughput capabilities of the BPDs vary by location.

Blood Transshipment

The U.S. military also possesses a unique capability to deploy manning and hardware for handling transshipment operations for blood in support of contingency operations. Owned by the Air Force, these Expeditionary Blood Transshipment Centers (EBTCs) act as the central receiving and shipment points for blood within a theater of operations. Each EBTC would be established at a large forward aerial port of debarkation, receiving its stock from the ASWBPLs and ultimately acting as a local distribution hub to provide blood to medical support operations farther forward.

EBTCs are scalable in their capability, ultimately expanding to an ability to store and distribute up to 3,000 units of blood per week. In terms of storage capacity, a full-scale EBTC can store 2,000 units of frozen blood and 1,000 units of refrigerated blood. While the Air Force owns and provides this capability, during contingency, EBTCs would fall under the operational control of the receiving Combatant Command's Joint Blood Program Office.

Forward Collection of Blood

The military also employs capabilities to collect and store blood in forward operating areas. These are generally referred to as Blood Support Detachments (BSDs). BSDs can receive blood shipments from EBTCs and are equipped to store and re-ice them to maintain appropriate temperatures. BSDs can operate in conjunction with BPDs to receive thawed blood as well. Furthermore, they can collect FWB to support emergency blood demands, such as the provision of blood for a surge in trauma patients after combat action. Some BSDs are also equipped with apheresis capabilities, affording them the specialized function of producing platelets for use at nearby MTFs.

The Air Force also has a deployable capability to fulfill the role of blood collection forward. Expeditionary Blood Support Centers (EBSCs) are manned and equipped to collect FWB and apheresis platelets in theater. The EBSC can act as a deployable lab team to augment larger expeditionary MTFs, such as an Air Force Theater Hospital or joint equivalent. To allow for storage at the point of collection, EBSCs also deploy with a small holding capacity of up to 60 units of FWB.

It is important to note that EBSCs are not equipped to test blood for pathogens. Consequently, an EBSC typically deploys to larger MTFs, such as an Air Force Theater Hospital, to leverage access to the broader array of blood testing capabilities available there. However, when EBSCs deploy to smaller operating locations without access to the labs or equipment to perform testing, the blood they collect is intended to be used only when other blood is unavailable and when blood transfusion is necessary to save a patient's life.

Organization of This Report

In the remainder of this analysis, we will explore a number of technologies and operational concepts that may offer promise for adding resiliency to the blood supply chain. These approaches will span a spectrum of technologies, from those that are available today to those that hold promise in the longer term. We will also examine analytic frameworks to assess their ability to add resiliency to the supply chain.

Next, Chapter Two will establish a fundamental framework for examining and assessing blood supply chain operations. Chapter Three explores approaches that touch on collection and transportation of blood, collectively referred to as operations in the supply chain that are "upstream" from local storage at an individual MTF. In Chapter Four, we will turn our focus to support at forward operating locations, including blood storage, expiration, and demand (collectively known as "downstream" operations). In Chapter Five, we evaluate how planners might assess the utility of resiliency of mitigations. Finally, we conclude in Chapter Six with some summary remarks and recommendations for future operation of the Joint blood supply chain.

The list of approaches and technologies we will explore in this text is by no means intended to be exhaustive. Rather, we hope to provide a useful set of examples possessing characteristics of fractionation, composition, and functional substitution that will touch on several temporal and spatial scales for their implementation. Our intent is to expose readers to a variety of constructs and capabilities to stimulate thought and discussion toward achieving greater resiliency in the blood supply chain. Ultimately, through greater resiliency in blood operations, the medical support network could see improved patient outcomes under a wider array of system stressors and threat conditions.

CHAPTER TWO

Developing a Blood Supply Chain Framework

We have provided an overview of blood components and the supply chain elements employed in the collection, testing, processing, shipment, storage, and transfusion of blood. When viewed from the vantage point of the myriad individual products and operational capabilities, the blood supply chain may at first appear as a complex array of specialized commodities and detailed logistics processes. To aid in supply chain assessment, it will prove beneficial to shift focus and to alter our perspective, examining the blood supply chain through a higher-level framework.

A Qualitative Supply Chain Framework

Rather than seeing the blood supply chain in terms of individual products or specialized capabilities, it can be helpful to generalize the system more broadly. As shown in Figure 2.1, we can cast the system as more fundamental flows of blood through a network that is oriented relative to the storage of blood products.

At the center of the figure is a representation of the storage of blood, whether frozen or liquid. Depending on the access to glycerolization capabilities at the local facility, it may be possible to convert between blood's frozen and liquid states. Leading into the local blood storage facility is a portrayal of blood flowing into that storage hub. Blood could be transported from sources far off-site, or it could be derived from sources closer to the point of storage. Finally, the figure provides a construct for the movement of blood out of local storage. Blood could be moved to support downrange needs, be transfused for local blood demands, or even expire, departing the supply chain as it ages beyond its viable shelf-life. It is also worth noting that the figure distinguishes between the demand for blood and the amount that is available for patient use. In some circumstances, the demand signal may outstrip the on-hand supply. Hence, it is important to be able to capture when these mismatches might occur so that circumstances leading to unsatisfied demand for blood can be identified and mitigated.

What this representation of the blood supply chain then affords is a way of looking at the problem through a variety of perspectives. Those vantage points can even vary, relating to the spatial scale or temporal extent of a problem of interest. For example,

Figure 2.1
A Qualitative Framework of Blood Supply Chain Flows and Processes

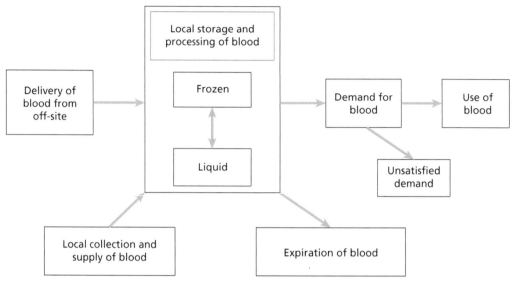

an analyst may be interested in thinking through supply chain behavior as it affects, say, a small MTF supporting a deployed brigade during a contingency operation. The tactical factors of interest at that scale might involve developing a better understanding of local blood demands. In turn, those demands can drive storage requirements and transportation schedules to ensure blood is available when needed. Similar examples spanning a variety of spatial and temporal scales are described in Table 2.1.

Similarly, the problem could be cast at a more strategic level. As shown in the center column of Table 2.1, a combatant command's blood planning group may need a framework to evaluate the requirements for blood support at a theaterwide level during large-scale combat operations. In this scenario, the central aspect of Figure 2.1 can represent the storage of blood integrated across the extent of the theater's network of MTFs. Core considerations driving the supply chain at this level of aggregation would be driven by a long-term understanding of casualty demands in the conflict, how they might drive the demand signal for blood, and how BDC and ASWBPL support will need to be mobilized to deliver an appropriate level of blood to support combat casualty needs.

Finally, depending on the fidelity of analysis required by a planner, it is certainly possible to recast the framework of Figure 2.1 as a daisy-chain of flows across a complex network of capabilities. In this fashion, a blood planner can represent supply chain processes, capturing day-by-day and MTF-by-MTF effects across the network. By building a high-resolution detailed network of flow processes, an analyst could cap-

Table 2.1
Characteristics of Support to the Blood Supply Chain from a Variety of Perspectives

		Brigade-Level Support for Trauma Surge	Theaterwide Blood Demand for Combat Support	ASWBPL Support to the Theater
Scale of support	Spatial extent	1s–10s of miles	100s–1,000s of miles	1,000s of miles
	Anticipated duration of support	Days to weeks	Months to years	Years
Flows for	Off-site transport	From BSD	From ASWBPL	From BDCs
	Local collection	Limited by availability of donors	As needed to augment supply	N/A
	Expiration	N/A	Limited, as on-hand supply meets ongoing demands	Minimized to limit wastage
	Blood demand	Low to high, relative to threat	Modest to high	Modest, as needed at treatment facilities
	Deglycerolization	N/A	As needed for demand satisfaction	As needed for training, testing
Blood supply	Liquid	Small	Large	Large
	Frozen	N/A	Modest to large	Large

ture the response level of diverse supply chain elements, including BDCs, ASWBPLs, BPDs, and transshipment hubs. At the product level, the network representation can also track multicommodity flows while capturing important product-level behavior over time, such as demand satisfaction rates and losses due to expiration.

Understandably, greater levels of detail in the fidelity of the representation of the blood supply chain can rapidly lead to a complex modeling representation. A high-level, strategic overview of theater processes may be feasible using back-of-the-envelope estimation, whereas detailed network representations may drive more sophisticated computational requirements. The important takeaway at this stage is that the supply chain framework here is sufficiently flexible to accommodate a variety of network compositions, be they more tactical, at the level of MTF operations, or more strategic, as cast at a regional or theater level.

Using the Blood Supply Chain Framework to Evaluate System Stressors

With this overarching view of capabilities, we can explore a variety of challenges that could stress supply chain operations. Here, using the qualitative representation shown in Figure 2.1, we will briefly explore three cases that have generated discussion recently in military and medical literature: mass casualty events, the outbreak of a pandemic, and large-scale combat operations. While only one of the three is necessarily tied to military operations, these examples afford the opportunity for a qualitative examination of blood supply chain operations through the lens of the framework discussed earlier.

Mass Casualty Events

In the wake of terror attacks or mass shooting events, medical facilities near the attack can be expected to see a significant surge in the influx of trauma patients. While not every victim of the attack will require a transfusion, the injury distributions stemming from bombings or small arms fire generally yield, on average, an overall expectation of three units of PRBC per patient admitted. It is important to note that this is the projected mean for PRBC use. Based on an analysis of recent mass casualty events, five PRBC units per admission can be expected at the 90th percentile of the demand distribution.[1] It is worth noting that the mean expectation of three PRBCs per casualty here mirrors experience in combat operations. In one such examination, the planning factor of three units approximates requirements for blood support to Israeli forces injured in conflict operations ranging from the wars in Lebanon in 1982 and 2006 to 2014's Operation Protective Edge in Gaza.[2]

To promote optimal outcomes for severe trauma patients, recent analysis also suggests that a mixture of blood products should be delivered, following between a 1:1:1 and a 2:1:1 ratio of PRBC:plasma:platelets.[3] With these projections for patient demand signals, one might imagine how blood support would be challenged at a

---

[1]   G. Ramsey, "Blood Component Transfusions in Mass Casualty Events," *Vox Sanguinis*, Vol. 112, 2017, pp. 648–659.

[2]   E. Shinar, "Be Prepared: Blood Centre Preparedness Plan in Disasters," presented at AABB Annual Meeting, October 7, 2017, San Diego, Calif. (The AABB was formerly known as the American Association of Blood Banks.)

[3]   One such study is the Pragmatic Randomized Optimal Platelet and Plasma Ratio (PROPPR) trial, as documented in J. B. Holcomb, B. C. Tilley, S. Baraniuk, E. E. Fox, C. E. Wade, J. M. Podbielski, D. J. del Junco, K. J. Brasel, E. M. Bulger, R. A. Callcut, M. J. Cohen, B. A. Cotton, T. C. Fabian, K. Inaba, J. D. Kerby, P. Muskat, T. O'Keeffe, S. Rizoli, B. R. Robinson, T. M. Scalea, M. A. Schrieber, D. M. Stein, J. A. Weinberg, J. L. Callum, J. R. Hess, N. Matiievic, C. N. Miller, J. F. Pittet, D. B. Hoyt, G. D. Pearson, B. Leroux, G. van Belle, and the PROPPR Study Group, "Transfusion of Plasma, Platelets, and Red Blood Cells in a 1:1:1 vs. a 1:1:2 Ratio and Mortality in Patients with Severe Trauma," *Journal of the American Medical Association*, Vol. 313, No. 5, 2015, pp. 471–482. It is important to note that the reference point for platelet dosing here is the volume of platelets that can

small, individual MTF. A smaller facility, for example, may have storage capacity for only 50 PRBC units—a capacity that may satisfy the demand for support to only 15 or 20 admissions.

Thinking of the processes and flows in Figure 2.1, we can visualize the core system stressor as coming from the end-user demand for blood. This could necessitate significant demand on stores at a hospital receiving the load of trauma patients. Where potential backfill is needed, regional blood banks may be able to handle any stockouts at individual MTFs. Blood expiration is likely to be of little concern, as the temporal extent of trauma patients arriving at the hospital would be far shorter than the shelf life of the blood needed to support them. Finally, obtaining additional supply from an emergency blood drive would likely be late to the need. Here, collection and testing of blood from the drive would likely take more time than is available to support a surge of rapidly arriving trauma patients.

Analysis of historical data bears out these higher-level observations on supply chain behavior. Several studies have explored outcomes from a variety of mass casualty events, ranging among the London subway bombing of 2005, the Boston Marathon bombing of 2013, the Paris terrorist attack of 2015, and the Orlando nightclub shooting of 2016.[4] These analyses have shown that the most valuable blood supplies were those on the shelf at the receiving hospitals during the surge in trauma patients. When a local supply of blood began to dwindle, dispatchers could route stock to individual hospitals in need from locations where supply was available. Volunteer donations did not help in the immediate aftermath of the mass casualty event. Rather, volunteerism helped to rapidly replenish stock once the crisis had passed.

Consequently, while historical mass casualty events have certainly stressed the supply chain, the freedom of movement to transport supplies coupled with access to ample on-hand stock has proven a valuable combination in reacting to short-term demand surges. Nonetheless, historical examples may not be indicators of future outcomes for the blood supply chain, as system performance is a function of the number of patients received across the MTF network. Larger-scale casualty counts, especially when they arrive at MTFs over a short period, could stress the supply chain to a point where patient needs for blood would go unmet.

---

be produced from a unit of whole blood. In comparison, a unit of platelets drawn by apheresis methods generates between four and six times the count derived from whole blood.

[4]   In addition to Ramsey, 2017, outcomes from these mass casualty events are detailed in Karen Quillen, "Blood Use After the Boston Marathon Bombing April 2013," presented at AABB Annual Meeting, San Diego, Calif., October 7, 2017; and Pierre Tiberghien, "Mass Casualty Events: Blood Bank and Transfusion Service Perspective—The November 13th, 2015 Paris Attacks," presented at AABB Annual Meeting, San Diego, Calif., October 7, 2017.

Pandemic Outbreak

Recent analysis has suggested another potentially significant stressor to the blood supply chain: pandemic.[5] In the scenario explored by Mulcahy et al. (2016), the authors posited that a large-scale outbreak of a pathogen such as influenza could influence the rate at which donors would be able to provide blood. For example, a large portion of the traditional donor base would be highly unlikely to consider donation while ill. Furthermore, in the case of an emergent pathogen, time may be required to deploy appropriate tests to detect the disease in a donated unit of blood. Consequently, blood banks would likely opt to defer a donor's eligibility to provide blood until such a time as detection of the pathogen is possible.

Here, we picture a significantly different scenario from that posited for a mass casualty event. Through Figure 2.1's framework, in the case of pandemic, the long-term demand projections for blood may be relatively consistent with historical steady-state usage rates.[6] However, with a drawdown in the donation rate for blood entering the system, the supply chain may need to operate on reserve stocks of blood over protracted periods. The problem of access to available supply would be exacerbated over time, especially as blood in storage reaches its useful shelf-life and expires.

Large-Scale Combat Operations

Finally, we turn our attention to an example of significant salience to the military's blood supply chain: large-scale combat. One scenario that is viewed as especially stressing is the possibility of conflict against a peer or near-peer adversary who can generate a contested, degraded, or operationally limited (CDO) combat environment. Over the past few decades, the defense community has taken increasing note of potential adversaries across the globe who have focused significant research into the development of long-range, high-precision conventional missile capabilities. In the employment of these missile systems across a theater of operations, an adversary could significantly degrade the freedom of movement for U.S. forces by targeting military infrastructure such as command and control centers, runways, and fuel depots.[7] The widespread

---

[5]   This scenario is covered in Andrew W. Mulcahy, Kandice A. Kapinos, Brian Briscombe, Lori Uscher-Pines, Ritika Chaturvedi, Spencer R. Case, Jakub Hlavka, and Benjamin M. Miller, *Toward a Sustainable Blood Supply in the United States: An Analysis of the Current System and Alternatives for the Future*, Santa Monica, Calif.: RAND Corporation, RR-1575-DHHS, 2016. Of three scenarios examined—natural disaster, terrorist attack, and pandemic—the pandemic scenario was deemed to pose the highest risk to the national blood supply chain.

[6]   In fact, demand may even decrease relative to historical norms. For example, during the outbreak, patients across a regional network or catchment area may choose to postpone elective surgical procedures, limiting the need for transfusion services.

[7]   Readers may have also encountered the term *anti-access/area denial* (A2/AD) to describe a conflict environment of this nature. The defense community has recently begun to pivot from the use of A2/AD to CDO. A2/AD has connotations of an inability to move into or within a theater of military operations, whereas CDO better suggests a degraded freedom of movement.

occurrence of blast events would also likely generate significant numbers of casualties, many of whom would have severe trauma injuries.

In terms of the blood supply chain framework, such a scenario could indeed significantly degrade the ability of the military to provide blood to combat casualties. The generation of the CDO environment through prolonged missile strikes across a theater of military operations would yield a long-term, large-scale demand signal for blood. These same strikes could significantly degrade operations at airfields that have come under attack. In so doing, the adversary might be capable limiting the timely movement of blood into the theater through the traditional supply chain flows through the BDCs, ASWBPLs, and EBTCs. As the conflict wears on, blood in local storage at MTFs across the theater could be depleted, leading to challenges in providing sufficient quantities to combat casualties.

Adding Resiliency to the Blood Supply Chain

In the earlier discussion of the military's blood supply chain, we observed a relatively streamlined supply chain operation. Based on a model predicated on the free flow of information, ready access to transportation, and a widespread donor base, blood can follow a linear path in vein-to-vein supply chain operations. In thinking through global distribution, blood begins with its collection at the BDCs, flows through the ASWBPLs for processing and shipment, and potentially routes through transshipment hubs on its way to BPDs and BSDs, eventually being stored at forward MTFs to support patient demands.

However, the example of large-scale combat operations in a CDO environment yields conditions under which performance of the blood supply chain could be significantly degraded. In thinking about the Joint system, individual capabilities in the overall chain can offer impressive capabilities. However, these capabilities—especially those that must be transported and set up prior to their use, such as expeditionary MTFs, EBTCs, and EBSCs—can require significant time in their deployment and setup before they achieve full operational capability. Similarly, fixed-facility operations, such as the BDCs and ASWBPLs, may require time to acquire personnel augmentation in time of crisis to ramp up existing capabilities. Furthermore, transportation of blood across the globe is predicated on facile access to sufficient resources such as military airlift assets, including C-130s and C-17s.

In light of the challenges that might eventuate in the military's future combat environments, the defense community has begun to explore alternative capabilities, technologies, and concepts of operation that might afford additional flexibility in military operations. To that end, the Defense Advanced Research Projects Agency (DARPA) stood up a program known as the Complex Adaptive System Composition and Design Environment (CASCADE). In this program, researchers are developing novel mathematical frameworks to explore approaches for augmenting operational resiliency.

For the analysis here, we examined potential challenges to the Joint blood supply chain through the lens of this program. While we do not address the specifics of any particular mathematical constructs in this research, we do focus on the integration of three resiliency principles central to the CASCADE effort: fractionation, composition, and functional substitution:[8]

- *Fractionation* enables the scaling of elements within the supply chain to deploy capabilities relative to the level of their need farther downrange. It may be important to expedite the deployment of a small expeditionary capability to pave the way for follow-on augmentation capabilities. For example, a small EBSC could be rapidly deployed and employed until a larger BSD could be established.
- *Composition* supports the tailoring of capabilities to best meet downrange needs. For example, a small Army medical brigade does not typically deploy with equipment for deglycerolization operations. The Air Force does have a small deployable capability, the Frozen Blood Product Team (FBPT), with the appropriate hardware and staffing, storage, thawing, and deglycerolization of FRBC. Under some circumstances, it may prove useful to deploy an FBPT in concert with the Army brigade.
- *Functional substitution* looks for opportunities to amend currently used stocks and capabilities with substitutes better tailored to operational needs. For example, medical research and development could be targeted to provide approaches and technologies to replace short-lived blood products with longer-lasting alternatives.

The military's operational community also offers insights on ways to think about resiliency. In the operational context, military planners seek mechanisms to ensure that operations can be sustained in the face of system stressors, such as when a base or deployed unit comes under attack during combat. Here, planners often think about three principles: redundancy, durability, and reparability.[9] Independent of the principles one applies in developing a plan to promote resiliency, with access to a broader

---

[8]   The blood supply chain analysis presented here is supported by CASCADE's agile medicine thread, where performers are applying sophisticated modeling techniques to explore mechanisms to add resiliency to deployed military medical operations. CASCADE currently has two other active threads exploring military logistics (focusing on resupply) and command and control operations (focusing on search and rescue processes). For more on CASCADE, refer to DARPA, "Advancing the Design and Modeling of Complex Systems," press release, Arlington, Va., November 20, 2015.

[9]   *Redundancy* is the capability to quickly employ a substitute should a primary asset be damaged or destroyed, mirroring functional substitution as described earlier. *Durability* is the construct of having access to assets that can withstand adversary attack. For blood support, durability ties to the ability to better withstand surges, such as having more blood on hand to bear the brunt of demand spikes. Finally, reparability involves the ability to rapidly reconstitute an entity that has been damaged or is otherwise in need of repair. For the blood supply chain, this can

portfolio of mitigation technologies, strategies, and concepts of operation, the military blood supply chain would be better equipped to plan for and react to system stressors. In so doing, more linear—and potentially brittle—supply chain operations could be augmented, enhanced, and improved to achieve greater resiliency.

Conclusions

In this chapter, we presented a framework useful in the examination of the blood supply chain. The framework allows for the qualitative comparison of inputs and outputs of blood through an MTF, comparing the relative magnitudes between the delivery of blood from off-site, access from local sources, availability of on-hand stock, rate of wastage, and the demand for and use of blood by patients. In some circumstances, such as large-scale combat operations in contested operating environments, the satisfaction of end-user demand may be restricted by one or more elements in the supply chain. To ensure resilient access to safe blood in the face of such stressors, it can be important to consider the addition of mitigation measures to the blood supply chain. In the next chapter, we will begin to explore some of these mitigations, beginning with resiliency measures that influence supply and delivery of blood to an MTF, more generally referred to as elements of the blood supply chain "upstream" from the treatment facility.

---

tie to having ready access to biomedical equipment maintainers and spare parts to rapidly repair malfunctioning apheresis hardware.

CHAPTER THREE
Enhancing Upstream Resiliency of the Blood Supply Chain

In the last chapter, we developed a fundamental framework for thinking about flows of blood into and through the military's blood supply chain. Within that framework, a key aspect of supply chain operations is the provision of blood for storage at MTFs around the globe. Typically, blood is shipped overseas from the ASWBPLs in the continental United States, though the ASBP does operate some BDCs abroad. By and large, shipments to smaller MTFs are managed by airlift, including military cargo aircraft such as C-130s and C-17s. However, there may be circumstances, including mass casualty events or large-scale combat operations, that could place so much stress on traditional supply chain operations that blood becomes unavailable to the patients who need it. In this chapter, we will examine several mechanisms that offer promise in adding resiliency to the delivery and collection of blood to these MTFs.

Augmenting Blood Delivery by Airdrop or Unmanned Aerial Vehicle

Depending on the nature of the conflict or disaster, the quantities of blood required, and the distances between storage facilities and MTFs, the use of unmanned aerial vehicles (UAVs) to deliver blood may be an effective alternative in a CDO environment. Currently, the nonprofit startup Zipline is using UAVs to deliver blood in Rwanda, where road access between the storage facility and medical center may not be reliable or offer a timely option.[1] The lithium-ion battery–powered Zipline UAVs, known as "zips," can currently carry 1.5 kg of payload (approximately three units apiece of PRBC and plasma) and can travel a radius of 75 km at 100 km/hr, making its delivery in under an hour. Operators use a catapult to launch a fixed-wing UAV, which then para-

---

[1]   Zipline also has an agreement with Tanzania to begin UAV distribution of blood products and other medical products, such as vaccines, antimalarials, and sterile intravenous tubing. Distribution is set to begin in 2018. For more on the enterprise, readers may refer to Aryn Baker, "The American Drones Saving Lives in Rwanda," *Time*, 2017; Dan Simmons, "Rwanda Begins Zipline Commercial Drone Deliveries," BBC News, October 14, 2016; and Lawrence Williams, "Just in Time Blood Delivery," presented at AABB Annual Meeting, San Diego, Calif., October 7, 2017.

chutes the product to the destination. Delivery is precise, as the target area for each zip drop is about the size of two automobile parking spaces.

While UAVs offer opportunity for autonomous delivery from a centralized repository of blood, it may be more advantageous to launch blood deliveries from a mobile platform. With use of an airborne asset, such as a military cargo aircraft, the aircraft itself can serve as a mobile warehouse to provide deliveries to several dispersed operating locations. However, in a CDO environment, landing access to airstrips may be significantly degraded. In such a circumstance, it is possible to airdrop a full pallet of blood by low-altitude parachute extraction (LAPE) or by using the Joint Precision Airdrop System. In this fashion, as many as 2,500 units of PRBC packed in ice can be delivered to a single operating location.[2]

In operating environments where the airspace near a delivery zone is contested, it may also be possible to deliver blood supplies by glider. In one effort designed to explore that possibility, DARPA's Inbound, Controlled, Air-Releasable, Unrecoverable Systems (ICARUS) program promoted the development of a glider system that could be launched during flight from military cargo aircraft. The ICARUS gliders were designed to carry payloads between 2 and 20 pounds, traveling upward of 50 miles to their target site. Moreover, some designs for these gliders were developed to biodegrade within hours of deployment, leaving no trace of the glider platform itself. While this capability would be of distinct utility for the medical resupply of covertly deployed Special Operations Forces (SOF), glider-based resupply in general could also offer a meaningful mechanism for resupply to austere operating locations.[3] Similarly, the U.S. Marine Corps has been developing its tactical air delivery (TACAD) glider, a wooden asset capable of delivering 700 pounds of cargo.[4]

The Zipline experience, ICARUS, and the TACAD program offer examples of the innovative use of unmanned capabilities to deliver blood in CDO environments. Technology is advancing at such a rate that these models offer but a few of many possible unmanned modes to deliver blood supplies. There are some trade-offs in their design, but UAVs can generally be adapted to meet most requirements for just-in-time blood delivery. Some of these trade-off/decision spaces include

- *payload versus distance versus time:* In general, a larger payload means a shorter range and possibly a longer delivery time, potentially driving the need for a larger

---

[2]   Headquarters, Departments of the Army and the Air Force, "Airdrop of Supplies and Equipment: Rigging Whole Blood," Field Manual 10-562, Technical Order 13C7-34-1, Washington, D.C., May 23, 1989.

[3]   The ICARUS capability has been released by DARPA and is currently under further development by Otherlab, where the system is now termed the Aerial Platform Supporting Autonomous Resupply Actions (Otherlab, "Industrial Paper Airplanes for Autonomous Aerial Delivery," press release, San Francisco, Calif., January 12, 2017).

[4]   The Marines will begin field testing TACAD assets in 2018 (Evan Ackerman, "U.S. Marines Testing Disposable Delivery Drones," *IEEE Spectrum*, April 17, 2017).

delivery platform. Depending on the projected demands of the scenario, this trade-off can prove critical. If there is a high demand for blood, a larger payload might be prioritized over a long range; if a longer distance is expected, a smaller payload with more trips or using a larger fleet might afford the better solution.

- *refrigeration and cooling needs:* Depending on ambient air temperature and time in flight, not all blood would require active or passive cooling mechanisms. If required to keep blood at appropriate temperatures, the size and weight needed for passive cold chain management can decrease payload capacity, while active management can both decrease payload and drive larger onboard energy requirements.

- *round trip versus one way:* UAVs may or may not need to be reused. This will be a function of the number of available UAVs, distance, payload, and the demand for blood. If UAVs are needed for multiple trips, planners must pay special attention to energy utilization, especially if batteries require a recharge or swap, or if a specific fuel is needed for the UAV. If ground-launched glider platforms are preferred, launching catapults will be needed at each launch and recovery site to enable round-trip journeys for the delivery assets.

- *receipt capabilities at the destination:* Where time, distance, or terrain considerations for UAV operation might prohibit the parachuting of blood, fixed-wing UAVs require a landing strip. Alternatively, UAVs can be designed to deploy with hover capabilities or with vertical landing/takeoff capabilities.

- *Global Positioning System (GPS) availability/guidance requirements:* Depending on situational need and permissivity of the operating environment, planners must consider access to and availability of GPS signal to aid in the navigation of the UAV asset.

- *noise restrictions:* Under many operational conditions, noise restrictions are not expected to be a limiting factor in UAV operation. However, a requirement for covert delivery of medical resupply in some military operations may drive the choice in delivery platform away from powered UAVs and toward glider assets.

- *cost:* As with all product development, there is often a cost trade-off between capacity, capability, and durability. A disposable UAV or a platform design that requires significant vehicle redundancy should ultimately be less expensive than a higher-capacity or more durable asset.

While UAVs are not currently in use by the U.S. Department of Defense for blood delivery, the technology is at a point where developing an appropriate vehicle to meet planning requirements could be relatively straightforward. Consequently, UAV delivery of blood could prove to be a reasonable solution in a CDO environment, depending on projected distance, demand, and time requirements.

Implementing Whole Blood Collection Protocols

FWB is generally not the product of choice in transfusion therapy, as the use of individual components allows the medical provider to tailor the delivery of products best suited to each individual patient's specific medical needs. However, there is a growing body of literature that demonstrates strongly positive outcomes for severe-trauma patients receiving FWB therapy.[5] It is important to note that, in the transfusion of FWB in a forward operating environment, several risks may come into play. These factors include the risk of transfusion-transmitted infection in the absence of tested FWB; bacterial contamination of the blood during storage in the field environment; and the need to transfuse FWB that is specific to the patient's blood type.[6]

In large-scale combat operations with a significant trauma casualty load, however, whole blood therapy may be needed to satisfy the total demand for blood. Consequently, as an emergency means for developing a stock of blood at a forward operating location, the local medical commander may call for whole blood collection from the base's population of military personnel. This protocol is often referred to as mobilization of the "walking blood bank" (WBB). The U.S. Army Institute for Surgical Research emphasizes caution in the execution of these protocols, specifically stating that

> [i]t is NOT appropriate, as a matter of convenience, to use FWB as an alternative to more stringently controlled blood products for patients who do not have severe, immediately life-threatening injuries. FWB is to be used only when other blood products are unable to be delivered . . . when specific stored components are not available . . . or when stored components are not adequately resuscitating a patient with an immediately life-threatening injury.[7]

---

[5] A primary consideration here is that, as was demonstrated in the PROPPR trial, patients suffering from massive hemorrhage tend to benefit from a ratio of about 1:1:1 PRBC:plasma:platelets during transfusion, which is the natural component ratio in FWB. For more, refer to P. C. Spinella, J. G. Perkins, J. G. Grathwohl, A. C. Beekley, and J. G. Holcomb, "Warm Fresh Whole Blood Is Independently Associated with Improved Survival for Patients with Combat-Related Traumatic Injuries," *Journal of Trauma*, Vol. 66, 2009, pp. S69–S76; and J. G. Perkins, A. P. Cap, P. C. Spinella, A. F. Shorr, A. C. Beekley, K. W. Grathwohl, F. J. Rentas, C. E. Wade, and J. B. Holcomb, "Comparison of Platelet Transfusion as Fresh Whole Blood Versus Apheresis Platelets for Massively Transfused Combat Trauma Patients," *Transfusion*, Vol. 51, No. 2, February 2011, pp. 242–252.

[6] Many readers may be familiar with blood typing, also known as the ABO system. A patient's blood group (O, A, B, or AB) is identified along with its Rh factor (present [+] or negative [–]). To limit the risk of a negative transfusion reaction, such as hemolysis, it is important that a donor unit be compatible with the patient's own blood group and Rh factor. In general, group O blood can be safely donated to all patients, while group AB patients can safely receive blood of all types. For safety, it is important to type and cross-match donor blood with the patient's to ensure no risk of adverse reaction.

[7] U.S. Army Institute of Surgical Research, "Joint Theater Trauma System Clinical Practice Guideline: Fresh Whole Blood (FWB) Transfusion," October 24, 2012.

If medical planners expect the possible need to mobilize a WBB, it is important to ensure that adequate supplies are on hand ahead of time to assist in the collection and testing of FWB. This should include not only blood bags, but sufficient needles, tubing, and storage for any blood to be refrigerated. Where possible, rapid testing kits should be on hand for ABO/Rh typing and identification of pathogen vectors such as HBV, HCV, and HIV. Moreover, sample vials should be in stock to collect aliquots of donated blood for further testing after the WBB event, once laboratory access is available.

It is important to note that, in steady state, the rate of collection from the WBB will be driven by the size of its population. Recall from the earlier discussion in Chapter One that donors are generally able to provide a unit of FWB only once every 56 days. For example, if 1,000 deployed service members donated in a pattern spread out evenly over each 56-day window, the WBB could collect fewer than 18 units per day.[8] Depending on expected demands for blood, this may be enough to offer sufficient supply, especially in scenarios where steady-state demands are modest or when sudden, one-time spikes in demand may require surge collection for rapid replenishment.

However, if needed, it may be possible to accelerate that rate of collection. A protein known as erythropoietin, secreted by the kidney, stimulates the production of red blood cells in the bone marrow. Compounds related to erythropoietin, such as epoetin alfa, can be produced in cell culture and injected in a patient to stimulate the same effect. After activation of the WBB, epoetin alfa could be delivered to volunteer soldiers of type O to accelerate their production of red cells. This would contract their interdonation interval, increasing the overall rate at which FWB could be produced. However, analysis would be warranted to determine appropriate dosing levels for epoetin alfa and the effective rate at which the volunteer soldiers could donate.[9] Prior research has shown that this mechanism can prove effective, though iron supplementation in the donor pool may be necessary for greatest benefit.[10]

---

[8]   Recall that type O donors are the most desirable, given the relative safety of their blood during transfusion. In the general U.S. population, between 40 and 45 percent of donors are type O. Consequently, in this example of a 1,000-person donor pool, the expectation is that only about eight units per day would be type O.

[9]   It is worth mentioning that compounds such as epoetin alfa are typically refrigerated. Thus, not only would the intended use of these products require advance planning to assess desired on-hand stock levels, but it will also emphasize the need for ongoing cold chain management in their transport and storage.

[10]   This procedure has been tested with patients donating blood intended for their own use in surgery (known as autologous donation) (F. Mercuriali, A. Zanella, G. Barosi, G. Inghilleri, E. Biffi, A. Vinci, and M. T. Colotti, "Use of Erythropoietin to Increase the Volume of Autologous Blood Donated by Orthopedic Patients," *Transfusion*, Vol. 33, No. 1, January 1993, pp. 55–60).

Sourcing Blood from Partner Nations

Currently, the Department of Defense considers the blood supplies in a few partner nations to be of sufficient quality as to be considered comparable to FDA compliance, including those of the United Kingdom, Canada, and the Netherlands.[11] With this exempt status for these nations' blood supplies, U.S. recipients of their blood obviate a requirement for follow-up medical examination to assess whether adverse consequences were associated with the transfusion. While this determination can help simplify international sourcing with select partners, there is no guarantee that the partner nations will have the appropriate quantities of blood on hand when there is need. Furthermore, if the partner nation faces civilian or military casualties of its own citizens or military service members, it is unlikely that U.S. defense forces could expect priority blood support.

However, in a conflict environment with limited access to traditional blood supply lanes from the United States, international sources may become crucial in the provision of blood. While only a few partners have official recognition for the quality of their blood supply, it is possible that safety risks associated with sourcing from nonpreapproved countries could be deemed acceptable by U.S. military leadership, especially in the context of large-scale combat operations. To help in the assessment of risk from pathogens in international blood supplies, the World Health Organization routinely publishes data documenting the safety and testing requirements of 156 nations.[12] This report documents a variety of factors related to global blood supplies, including the fraction of international blood donations that screen positive across a range of pathogens, as shown in Table 3.1.

While these data reflect the prevalence of common transfusion-transmitted diseases, it is important to note that they do not reflect outcomes across the full slate of vectors screened pursuant to FDA standards, including Chagas and HTLV. The data do suggest, that, on average, there is a nonzero risk of possible transfusion-related transmission of disease and that this risk can become significant, especially during a large blood transfusion. However, to save a patient who would otherwise die of his injuries in the absence of a transfusion, a medical provider may be willing to provide that patient with potentially contaminated blood. Ultimately, this is a balance of risk that the medical provider would have to weigh, but it is one that can be informed by analysis of prevalence statistics and the quality of life that the patient may expect in the aftermath of treatment.

---

[11] Jonathan Woodson, "Policy on the Establishment of Comparability of Foreign Nation Blood Supplies to Food and Drug Administration Compliant Blood Products," Health Affairs Policy Memorandum 11-008, Office of the Assistant Secretary of Defense for Health Affairs, Washington, D.C., July 11, 2011.

[12] One installment is World Health Organization, *Global Status Report on Blood Safety and Availability 2016*, Geneva, Switzerland, 2017.

Table 3.1
Median Pathogen Prevalence in International Blood Donations, by Country Income Group

Country Income Group	HIV (%)	HBV (%)	HCV (%)	Syphilis (%)
High	0.003	0.03	0.02	0.05
Upper middle	0.08	0.39	0.21	0.31
Lower middle	0.20	1.60	0.40	0.58
Low	1.08	3.70	1.03	0.90

SOURCE: World Health Organization, 2017.

NOTES: Incidence of vectors can be expected to vary not only by region and income class, but over time as well. For example, as utilization of the HBV vaccine for newborns becomes more common around the world, a larger population of those who are immune will age into the global donor pool and help to drive down the virus's incidence. Greater fidelity on these reported values is available in the World Health Organization report, including interquartile ranges for each entry in the table, as well as more detailed information on the prevalence of HIV in sub-Saharan Africa.

The World Health Organization data in Table 3.1 also suggest that, while partner nations in the World Bank's high or upper-middle income brackets have relatively low prevalence of pathogens in their blood, partners in the low to lower-middle income tiers may benefit from targeted investment to improve the safety of their blood supply. Such an investment can be an important component of a larger strategy for global health engagement. In employing such a strategy, the United States can work with the partner nation's medical establishment to better understand where limiting factors in the provision of quality blood lie. The avenues for improved operation could stem from a wide range of blood supply chain elements, such as stock management, transportation, facility operation and availability, and availability of sufficiently trained staff.[13]

To this end, U.S. Indo-Pacific Command has recently worked with partners such as Cambodia and Laos to expand their access to facilities and laboratory equipment, as well as to train blood bank managers.[14] Consequently, these partners are now better equipped to manage products such as PRBC, FFP, and platelets, distributing them more efficiently through centralized management of blood bank operations. However, this degree of commitment to a partner should not be a one-time investment. Rather, the United States needs to view this as an opportunity for repeated engagement, factoring in resources for ongoing investment in the partner's access to lab reagents and

---

[13] Later in this report, we will explicitly address in greater detail another approach for enhancing blood safety: pathogen-reduction technology.

[14] As of 2016, the World Bank assessed both Cambodia and Laos as lower-middle income nations. For additional detail on the specifics of U.S. Indo-Pacific Command's engagement with Cambodia, refer to Hok Kimcheng, "Current Situation of Cambodian National Blood Transfusion Center," presented at AABB Annual Meeting, San Diego, Calif., October 8, 2017.

supplies, as well as the maintenance and modernization of laboratory equipment and assets. Longer-term goals can include plans for managing donor recruitment and for developing milestones to bring the partner up to desired accreditation standards.

Producing Red Blood Cells In Vitro

While some health and safety risks are associated with donor-sourced blood in partner nations, it may be possible to contract the development, supply, and storage of lab-grown blood with select partners. With stem cells in a bioreactor, artificially cultured RBCs can be produced in vitro. This family of procedures is considered a potential source of blood for rare blood types. Given the requirements for specialized laboratory equipment, facilities, and supplies, the technology is not at a state where it could be readily deployed for use in the expeditionary setting. However, the technology may be viable for use by partner nations that can leverage a highly trained biomedical labor pool. The United States may be able to develop joint ventures with these partners to secure access to stores of RBCs generated in vitro.

Given that the technology is relatively nascent, production costs tend to be high and offer restricted throughput. By current production methods, one unit of cultured RBCs costs approximately $8,300,[15] and the process takes approximately three to four weeks to grow a mass sufficient to constitute between one and two units of PRBC.[16] Relative to the cost and time lines for traditional collection and handling of PRBC, current approaches for the cultivation of lab-grown blood make this solution infeasible for the near term.[17]

Despite the current high cost and their unlikely entry into mainstream production methods in the near-to-mid term, lab-grown cells offer a wide range of benefits that warrant ongoing investment in the technology. In vitro manufacture of RBCs guarantees that the product is disease-free, regardless of where it was developed. Additionally, all manufactured RBCs can be engineered to be universal donors, so blood typing would no longer be a requirement for artificially produced RBCs. Finally, individual cultured RBCs are all the same age (compared with human-produced RBCs, which all vary in age due to their continuous production in the body). This suggests that cultured red blood cells would have a longer shelf life than donor-procured RBCs.[18] With

---

[15]   G. F. Rousseau, M.-C. Giarratana, and L. Douay, "Large-Scale Production of Red Blood Cells from Stem Cells: What Are the Technical Challenges Ahead?" *Biotechnology Journal*, Vol. 9, No. 1, 2014, pp. 28–38.

[16]   E. E. Bouhassira, "Concise Review: Production of Cultured Red Blood Cells from Stem Cells," *Stem Cells Translational Medicine*, Vol. 1, No. 12, 2012, pp. 927–933.

[17]   In comparison, the cost a hospital typically pays for PRBC collected by traditional means from a FWB donor is $250 per unit (Mulcahy et al., 2016).

[18]   It is worth noting, given that glycerolized RBCs can last for up to ten years, the shelf-life enhancement that may be achievable with lab-grown cells will not displace the role of FRBC as the long-lasting blood product of choice.

these potential benefits, sustained investment in research and development for in vitro RBC production could yield significant returns in the global medical community with the advent of pathogen-free, universally transfusable blood. Furthermore, as discussed in Chapter Two, should a large-scale outbreak of a new blood-borne pathogen appear (such as the discovery of HIV in the 1980s), widespread access to lab-grown blood could offer significant risk mitigation for the global blood supply.

Conclusions

In this chapter, we have discussed a variety of mitigations and approaches for improving resiliency upstream in the blood supply chain—namely, enhancing access to blood supplies and their delivery to MTFs. Some of these techniques are not routinely practiced in contemporary military operations, such as Cold War–era airdrop of pallets of blood. Other mechanisms are evolving technologies, such as stem cell–based production of RBCs in laboratory bioreactors. While promising in their capacity for risk mitigation and distributed access to blood supplies, nascent technologies will require further research and development to improve their cost-effectiveness. Other methods may incur some risk in their implementation, such as the activation of WBBs or utilization of a partner nation's blood supplies. Finally, we also explored the potential utility of alternate delivery platforms, such as UAVs. Existing technology here is sufficiently advanced that these assets can be designed or tailored for blood-delivery requirements relative to operational parameters, such as payload, distance, and speed.

In the next chapter, we will explore mitigations that offer promise for resiliency at the MTF, as well as at points of injury, also referred to as locations "downstream" of the treatment facility. We will also present aspects of the blood supply chain that fall somewhat outside the framework presented earlier in Chapter Two, examining resiliency measures that can aid in supply-chain risk management.

CHAPTER FOUR

Enhancing Local and Downstream Resiliency of the Blood Supply Chain

In the last chapter, we examined a range of mitigation approaches, technologies, and concepts of operation for enhancing and ensuring access to blood at MTFs around the globe. Once that blood arrives at a hospital or other medical facility, a variety of additional supply-chain processes engage to ensure safe handling of blood leading up to its transfusion. In this chapter, we will explore mitigations in these local and downstream operations that may offer important capabilities for adding resiliency to these critical links in the military's blood supply chain.

Expediting the Processing of Frozen Red Blood Cells

There are two blood products that can be stored in a frozen state: glycerolized RBCs and FFP. As discussed earlier in Chapter One, FRBC can last for up to ten years under appropriate storage conditions, and FFP can last for up to one year. To prepare FFP for transfusion, each unit must be thawed. Typically, this process occurs in a warm water bath, requiring about 45 minutes to thaw. Thawing FRBC follows a similar process, but each unit requires additional processing postthaw before it is safe for transfusion.

Once thawed, glycerolized RBCs must be processed through a specialized cell washer to remove glycerol. By typical planning factors, one technician operating three cell washers in parallel can deglycerolize 12 units in 12 hours.[1] The process, however, can encounter one of two potential failure modes. First, given the extremely low temperatures at which FRBC must be stored (below −65 degrees Celsius), the plastic bags in which the blood is stored can become brittle and rupture, rendering the unit unusable. Second, one pass through the cell-washing process may fail to remove a sufficient volume of glycerol from the unit, requiring a second pass through the washer.

By these current processing methods, to provide large quantities of deglycerolized RBCs quickly, an equivalently large array of cell washers and technicians may need to operate in parallel. As a potential alternative, recent research has explored the viabil-

---

[1] ASBP, "Joint Blood Program Handbook," Technical Manual 8-227-12, Washington, D.C., December 1, 2011.

ity of a new cell-washing process to accelerate deglycerolization. In this system, glycerolized RBCs would undergo a multistage cell-washing process using serial dilutions of saline. Furthermore, this process works in concert with a specialized membrane-filtration device. Early analysis of this approach has shown that it may be possible to deglycerolize a unit of RBCs in a matter of minutes rather than the time scale of hours required for current processing techniques.[2] Cell washers commonly used by the military cost tens of thousands of dollars apiece, so development of newer approaches may need to note this price point as a benchmark for cost-effectiveness.

As an example of the benefit of expedited deglycerolization, a large freezer for FRBC can hold upward of 700 units. By current planning factors for standard deglycerolization approaches, around-the-clock operation of a set of three deglycerolization units could process this volume into PRBC over the course of a month. With faster deglycerolization capabilities (or more standard equipment operating in parallel), the entire freezer's worth of blood could potentially be processed in under a week.

Finally, it is important to note that the use of FRBC can introduce a challenge related specifically to its core strength of long shelf-life. As awareness of risk of new diseases develops, additional testing may enter common practice that was not required when an FRBC unit was initially produced. An example of this occurred in 2007, when the FDA added *Trypanosoma cruzi*, which causes Chagas disease, to the roster of pathogens that should be screened for in blood. Consequently, FRBC units in storage, collected as early as 1997, had not been tested for the disease. Ultimately, testing occurred on an as-needed basis, as retroactively testing thousands of units of stored blood would have involved significant resources in materiel and manpower. Thus, large-scale reliance on FRBC reserves brings a risk that the Department of Defense could face added expense as protocols for blood safety continue to evolve.

Extending the Shelf-Life of Blood

While the long shelf-life of FRBC can lead to unanticipated challenges, other products in the blood supply chain could benefit significantly from a longer-lasting period of potency. As we first established in Chapter One, blood is inherently perishable. Management of potency-dated supplies can be challenging, requiring a careful balance based on demand trends, production rates, acquisition time lines, and storage availability. One goal for improving efficiency in stock management is the ability to produce longer-lasting blood. As discussed earlier, the long shelf-life of FRBC is the key driver behind the military's development of stockpiles. Stock-management practices for sus-

---

[2]   For more, refer to R. E. Lusianti, J. D. Benson, J. P. Acker, and A. Z. Higgins, "Rapid Removal of Glycerol from Frozen-Thawed Red Blood Cells," *Biotechnology Progress*, Vol. 29, No. 3, 2013, pp. 609–620, as well as R. E. Lusianti and A. Z. Higgins, "Continuous Removal of Glycerol from Frozen-Thawed Red Blood Cells in a Microfluidic Membrane Device," *Biomicrofluidics*, Vol. 8, No. 5, September 2014, pp. 54–124.

taining products with a ten-year potency greatly simplify the administration of large reserves. This allows for efficient management of strategic stockpiles that would be able to absorb large potential shocks in the demand for blood. In contrast, these efficiencies in stock management would be far harder to sustain with the six-week viability of typical liquid PRBC.

Freeze Dried Plasma

While experimentation with FRBC began in the 1950s, the development of alternative processing protocols for plasma were first explored in the wake of World War I. Research led to processes to dehydrate plasma to extend its viability, eventually resulting in freeze-dried plasma (FDP). FDP first began to find widespread use by U.S. forces in World War II. However, in 1968, its use was implicated in hepatitis outbreaks, at which point FFP replaced FDP as the safer product of choice for plasma sourcing. While FFP can be stored for up to a year, it must be stored at temperatures below −18 degrees Celsius to remain viable. With this requirement for active cold chain management, in certain operating environments, safe storage conditions for FFP may be challenging to maintain.[3] Research thus continued to explore mechanisms for ensuring that FDP could be produced safely.

Through incorporation of modern safety protocols, current-day production mechanisms for FDP offer a safe, easy-to-manage product that remains viable for two years—twice the period of potency for FFP. FDP can be reconstituted as a liquid in under five minutes through the addition of sterilized water. France has been using FDP for over two decades, and more than 230,000 units of FDP have been administered in French and German hospitals since 2007.[4] Through this extensive experience in recent years, medical practitioners consider FDP equivalent to FFP in its effectiveness and safety. In 2010, upon recognizing the successful use of FDP by allied forces in Iraq and Afghanistan, Admiral William McRaven requested the development of FDA-approved FDP for use by U.S. troops as quickly as possible.[5] Consequently, U.S. SOF have been authorized to employ French-developed FDP. FDA approvals for widespread use of U.S. manufactured product lines are expected by 2020.[6]

---

[3]   Office of the Surgeon General, *Emergency War Surgery*, Fourth Revision, Falls Church, Va.: U.S. Army, 2013.

[4]   M. Rottenstreich, I. Malka, E. Glassberg, O. Schwartz, and B. Tarif, "Pre-Hospital Intra-Osseous Freeze Dried Plasma Transfusion: A Case Report," *Disaster and Military Medicine*, Vol. 1, No. 8, 2015.

[5]   J. M. Soares, "USAMMDA and Freeze-Dried Plasma: A Story of Success," press release, U.S. Army, September 9, 2016.

[6]   Emery Dalesio, "U.S. Troops Get Freeze-Dried Plasma for Battlefield Bloodshed," Associated Press, November 30, 2017.

Cold Stored Platelets

Platelets are another product for which significant shelf-life extension is possible. FDA regulations currently permit storage of platelets under refrigerated conditions. Relative to room-temperature storage, refrigerated platelets can be stored up to 15 days—a threefold increase. However, as outlined in Chapter One, platelets are most commonly stored at room temperature. This practice stems from the fact that the stress of refrigeration tends to activate platelet-clotting function more quickly, and activated platelets, being near the end of their life cycle, are purged more rapidly from the body than inactivated platelets.[7] Consequently, use of refrigerated platelets can be problematic for patients who receive platelet transfusion for therapeutic purposes, such as in the treatment of thrombocytopenia.

On the other hand, the stress that refrigeration can place on platelets can lead to benefits for trauma patients. Through priming of the platelet, transfusion of cold-stored platelets into an actively bleeding patient can yield positive patient outcomes where rapid improvements in clotting function are the desired goal.[8] Furthermore, the threefold extension in shelf-life can lead to broader employment of platelets at forward MTFs, where potency time lines would be sufficiently long to ensure safe transit of platelet units under cold chain management.

Synthetic Oxygen Carriers

While mechanisms exist to generate shelf-life extensions for common blood products such as RBCs, platelets, and plasma using current technologies and approaches, there is considerable ongoing research and development to produce safe blood substitutes with an even longer shelf-life. The goal in the development of a hemoglobin-based oxygen carrier (HBOC) is the synthesis of a product that is universally compatible, safe from immunologic reaction, free of the possibility of transmission of pathogens during transfusion, and suitable for long-term storage, preferably in the absence of cold chain management. While an HBOC would not serve as a true blood substitute—lacking the ability to assist in typical whole blood functions such as coagulation and immune response—it would nonetheless be able to act as a surrogate oxygen carrier, substituting for PRBC transfusion in the absence of naturally derived products.

---

[7]   Lacey Johnson, Shereen Tan, Ben Wood, April Davis, and Denese C. Marks, "Refrigeration and Cryopreservation of Platelets Differentially Affect Platelet Metabolism and Function: A Comparison with Conventional Platelet Storage Conditions," *Transfusion*, Vol. 56, No. 7, July 2016, pp. 1807–1818. This paper also points out the potential for cryopreservation of platelets at temperatures comparable with those for storage of FRBC. However, these storage conditions are not suitable for most forward MTFs, so we do not believe this mitigation to be a strong candidate for consideration at more forward medical operations.

[8]   T. M. Getz, R. K. Montgomery, J. A. Bynum, J. K. Aden, H. F. Pidcoke, and A. P. Cap, "Storage of Platelets at 4°C in Platelet Additive Solutions Prevents Aggregate Formation and Preserves Platelet Functional Responses," *Transfusion*, Vol. 56, No. 6, 2016, pp. 1320–1328.

To date, despite decades of research in the capability, no HBOC has performed successfully in animal or human trials. HBOCs have been associated with a wide array of common side effects, including hypertension, neurotoxicity, elevated enzyme production in the liver and pancreas, and renal toxicity. The genesis of these negative outcomes, however, is poorly understood.[9] Despite these initial hurdles in development of the capability, biotechnology continues to press to advance the field, especially given how the benefits of a safe, synthetic product would transform the landscape of transfusion science.

Moreover, as discussed earlier in the context of in vitro RBC production in Chapter Two, the research and development community has a challenging price point to target. While they might be able to levy a premium for their potential gains in safety, HBOCs need to remain cost-competitive relative to naturally produced PRBCs, which U.S. hospitals typically procure at about $250 per unit. It is important to consider that this typical $250-per-unit price point accounts for a variety of factors, including the cost of collection, testing, processing, storage, and expected wastage due to expiration. The price point also accounts for such factors as the aggregate costs of laboratory facilities and equipment, depreciation, maintenance, and labor. Thus, while core benefits of HBOCs relate to their lower expiration rate and greater safety, these benefits may drive significant increases in the cost for specialized hardware and labor skills for production. The clinical community has echoed this sensitivity to cost; one team commented, "Developers of oxygen carriers need to consider these [PRBC costs] as maximum costs for institutions that might use these products."[10]

Interventions at the Point of Injury

We have focused on a variety of mitigations and operational concepts that are useful in the initial links of the military's blood supply chain. Under some circumstances, forward forces may need to leverage additional options, especially while taking casualties and when time is insufficient to reach blood supplies stored at the nearest MTF.

Buddy Transfusion

Combat operations in austere environments have led to the development of a "buddy donation" program for FWB donations given directly in the field from one service member to another. In the United States, this program is currently used only by SOF. Buddy donation consists of prescreened service members and operates in two stages.

---

[9] A. Alayash, "Blood Substitutes: Why Haven't We Been More Successful?" *Trends in Biotechnology*, Vol. 32, No. 4, April 2014, pp. 177–185.

[10] M. Scott, D. Kucik, L. Goodnough, and T. Monk, "Blood Substitutes: Evolution and Future Applications," *Clinical Chemistry*, Vol. 43, No. 9, 1997, pp. 1724–1731.

In the first stage, the donor engages in the safe self-collection of a unit of blood. In the second, that unit of warm FWB is subsequently transfused into a wounded service member in the field.

In terms of safety protocols, the prescreening of donors includes an assessment of standard blood donation risk factors prior to deployment, with follow-up screening every three months during deployment. ABO- and Rh-compatible donors are the first choice of buddy donors, followed by universal donors.[11] With sufficient time, on-site screening, serology, and cross-matching should be performed in the field. Buddy donation carries a higher risk of infection or disease transmission than traditional transfusion practices, but in a time-critical situation, the risk of infection may be outweighed by the life-saving potential of the transfusion.

In 2013, the Norwegian Naval Special Operation Command conducted a study to assess whether donor combat readiness is affected by in-field donation. Analysis indicated that there was no significant change in physical performance after the participants donated a unit of blood, and, as an operational metric, there was no significant observed difference in pre- and post-donation shooting performance. Overall, the study demonstrated the effectiveness of buddy transfusion training for nonmedics and the continuity of donor combat performance in healthy, well-trained soldiers.[12]

Approaches to Limit Hemorrhage

In addition to mechanisms for sourcing blood close to the point of injury, medics have a few options to limit the extent of hemorrhage. By limiting the rate of blood loss, a medic may be able to employ scarce blood resources with more patients, buying them time to ensure they might survive until they can reach the nearest MTF, whereupon they can receive more definitive care.

Chemical Means

One in-field option is the administration of tranexamic acid (TXA). TXA inhibits fibrinolysis, which is the enzymatic breakdown of blood clots. Fibrinolysis can be especially problematic in patients suffering from massive hemorrhage, where degraded clotting function puts the patient at even greater risk of significant blood loss.[13] While the

---

[11] For more on buddy donation and its protocols, refer to A. D. Fisher, E. A. Miles, A. P. Cap, G. Strandenes, and S. F. Kane, "Tactical Damage Control Resuscitation," *Military Medicine*, Vol. 180, No. 8, 2015, p. 869; and A. B. Beckett, J. Callum, L. T. da Luz, J. Schmid, C. Funk, E. Glassberg, and H Tien, "Fresh Whole Blood Transfusion Capability for Special Operations Forces," *Canadian Journal of Surgery*, Vol. 58, No. 3, Suppl. 3, June 2015, pp. S153–S156.

[12] For more on the protocols of the study, refer to G. Strandenes, H. Skogrand, P. C. Spinella, T. Hervig, and E. B. Rein, "Donor Performance of Combat Readiness Skills of Special Forces Soldiers Are Maintained Immediately After Whole Blood Donation," *Transfusion*, Vol. 53, No. 3, March 2013, pp. 526–530.

[13] A thorough summary of TXA usage with trauma patients is outlined in L. M. Napolitano, M. J. Cohen, B. A. Cotton, M. A. Schreiber, and E. E. Moore, "Tranexamic Acid in Trauma: How Should We Use It?" *Journal of Trauma and Acute Care Surgery*, Vol. 74, No., 6, 2013.

decrease in blood loss after administration of TXA likely varies across patients and conditions, some evidence exists that this decrease can be as great as 25 percent.[14] It may also be possible to dose soldiers on high-risk combat missions prophylactically, limiting blood loss in the expectation of eventual injury.[15]

A large-scale study published in 2013 examined the effectiveness of TXA in reducing mortality due to blood loss, with a pool of more than 20,000 trauma patients worldwide. The study, known as the CRASH-2 trial, demonstrated the cost-effectiveness of TXA if administered within the first three hours of injury.[16] Due in part to the findings of the CRASH-2 study, the Joint Theater Trauma System in 2014 added the use of TXA to its Clinical Practice Guidelines.[17]

Mechanical Methods

While TXA and buddy transfusion have proven effective for general blood loss, additional mitigations may be available for patients with blood loss from localized injuries. Military service members receive training in the use of a tourniquet, which can help in the reduction of blood loss from extremities until the patient can be seen by a practitioner at the nearest MTF. However, tourniquets offer no help in the event of injury to the abdomen or torso. Given the high frequency of injuries of this type in recent conflicts, especially due to bomb blasts and small arms fire, a DARPA program known as the Wound Stasis System (WSS) explored technologies capable of limiting blood loss from abdominal trauma.[18] To this end, Arsenal Medical, a partner in the WSS program, developed a two-part liquid polymer system that can be introduced into the patient's abdomen laparoscopically. The liquids react to form an expanding,

---

[14] J. Wong, H. el-Beheiry, Y. R. Rampersaud, S. Lewis, H. Ahn, Y. De Silva, A. Abrishami, N. Baig, R. J. McBroom, and F. Chung, "Tranexamic Acid Reduces Perioperative Blood Loss in Adult Patients Having Spinal Fusion Surgery," *Anesthesia and Analgesia*, Vol. 107, No. 5, November 2008, pp. 1479–1486.

[15] Such prophylactic administration does happen prior to some surgical interventions, but further study may be warranted to determine appropriate dosing, time lines, and safety in combat environments (I. Pabinger, I D. Fries, H. Schoechl, W. Streif, and W. Toller, "Tranexamic Acid for Treatment and Prophylaxis of Bleeding and Hyperfibrinolysis," *Wiener Klinische Wochenschrift*, Vol. 129, No. 9, 2017, pp. 303–316).

[16] I. Roberts, H. Shakur, T. Coats, B. Hunt, E. Balogun, L. Barnetson, L. Cook, T. Kawahara, P. Perel, D. Prieto-Merino, M. Ramos, J. Cairns, and C. Guerriero, "The CRASH-2 Trial: A Randomised Controlled Trial and Economic Evaluation of the Effects of Tranexamic Acid on Death, Vascular Occlusive Events, and Transfusion Requirement in Bleeding Trauma Patients," *Health Technology Assessment*, Vol. 17, No. 10, March 2013, pp. 1–79.

[17] U.S. Army Institute of Surgical Research, "Joint Theater Trauma System Clinical Practice Guideline: Prehospital Trauma Care in the Tactical Setting," November 24, 2014.

[18] Analysis of lethal hemorrhages due to combat action between 2001 and 2011 shows that 67 percent of these injuries are abdominal. B. J. Eastridge, R. L. Mabry, P. Seguin, J. Cantrell, T. Tops, P. Uribe, O. Mallett, T. Zubko, L. Oetjen-Gerdes, T. E. Rasmussen, F. K. Butler, R. S. Kotwal, J. B. Holcomb, C. Wade, H. Champion, M. Lawnick, L. Moores, and L. H. Blackbourne, "Death on the Battlefield (2001–2011): Implications for the Future of Combat Casualty Care," *Journal of Trauma and Acute Care Surgery*, Vol. 73, No. 6, 2012, pp. S431–S437.

conformal, hemostatic foam that provides compression to the abdominal region and seals bleeding vessels. The patient can then be transported to the MTF, where, during surgery, the foam can be incrementally removed and damaged organs can be operated on in a controlled fashion.[19]

Another mechanism for mechanically stanching the loss of blood from the torso involves the introduction of a special catheter into the femoral artery. At the tip of the catheter is a small balloon that can be inflated to effectively cap the aorta, halting blood flow beyond the point of inflation. As with the conformal foam approach, resuscitative endovascular balloon occlusion of the aorta (REBOA) is intended to be a temporary means for limiting blood loss from injuries to the chest, abdomen, or pelvis.[20] Once the patient arrives at the nearest MTF, a surgical provider can remove the REBOA and repair the damage to injured vessels and organs.

Bioelectrical Stimulus Approaches

Cutting-edge technology may provide an additional mitigation for battlefield hemorrhage. Over the past 15 years, medical researchers have explored the effects of electrical pulses applied to the vagus nerve. Through appropriate stimulus, the vagus nerve can signal the brain to increase the production of targeted neurotransmitters and other chemicals to achieve a number of desired medical outcomes. For example, multiple experiments have shown that stimulating the vagus nerve, using either mechanical or electrical means, can increase the body's antiinflammatory response, thus lowering rates of inflammation and infection.[21]

Medical research has since built upon this body of work to explore the potential of vagus stimulation to control hemorrhage. Sponsored by DARPA, the Feinstein Institute for Medical Research manipulated the vagus nerve to coerce the brain into sending a signal to the spleen.[22] As a result, platelets transiting the spleen received a stimulus to prime them for subsequent clotting action. To date, results have been published based on swine experiments, where both bleeding time and total blood loss were approximately halved with this targeted stimulation of the vagus nerve.[23]

---

[19]   Arsenal Medical's system is known as ResQFoam, as further outlined on their webpage (Arsenal Medical, "Foam System for Acute Hemorrhage," website, undated). The U.S. Army is funding its further development.

[20]   For more on the REBOA procedure and its safety, see N. Saito, H. Matsumoto, T. Yagi, Y. Hara, K. Hayashida, T. Motomura, H. Iida, H. Yokota, and Y. Wagatsuma, "Evaluation of the Safety and Feasibility of Resuscitative Endovascular Balloon Occlusion of the Aorta," *Journal of Trauma and Acute Care Surgery*, Vol. 78, No. 5, May 2015, pp. 897–904.

[21]   These experiments are summarized in J. R. Fritz and J. M. Huston, "The Neural Tourniquet," *Bioelectronic Medicine*, Vol. 1, 2014, pp. 25–29.

[22]   The research has since been spun off by the Feinstein Institute to a firm known as Sanguistat.

[23]   C. J. Czura, A. Schultz, M. Kaipel, A. Khadem, J. M. Huston, V. A. Pavlov, H. Redl, and K. J. Tracey, "Vagus Nerve Stimulation Regulates Hemostasis in Swine," *Shock*, Vol. 33, No. 6, June 2010, pp. 608–613.

Once appropriate protocols are developed for human subjects, to treat a trauma victim, the electrical stimulus could be administered in the field with a handheld device. Evidence to date shows that the augmented clotting potential can last 24 to 48 hours beyond the time of initial bioelectrical stimulus. Should there be advance warning of combat action, soldiers could thus potentially be prophylactically treated before facing injury. While the technology is actively undergoing research and development, if trials on human subjects ultimately prove safe and effective, this approach has significant potential to be a low-risk method to reduce hemorrhage in combat traumas.

Other Dimensions of Resiliency in the Blood Supply Chain

Throughout the discussion thus far, the considerations for resiliency have focused primarily on the access to and the availability of blood. However, we have not yet provided explicit consideration of at least two additional classes of mitigation: operational continuity and risk avoidance.

Operational Continuity

During steady-state operations, the supply chain often focuses on assurance that sufficient quantities of blood are collected, processed, tested, and transported to the end-user MTFs, ensuring that blood is safe and available. Largely assumed during day-to-day operations is the availability of two core functions in the supply chain: access to energy and information. Without these two key provisions, continuity in the steady, reliable operation of the blood supply chain can be disrupted, so plans should be in place to account for mechanisms to operate in and recover from interference in these domains.[24]

Energy Resiliency

Access to sufficient power to sustain active cold chain management is essential to sustain the viability and safety of blood. In recent work for the Air Force, analysts developed a framework for assessing resiliency in access to energy for military operating locations.[25] As one key mitigation, the analysis highlights value in acquiring additional diesel generators. Through access to locally generated power, both fixed facilities and deployable MTFs for field use may be better equipped to handle disruptions in access to energy. While many expeditionary medical capabilities deploy with generators,

---

[24] These disruptions can be especially challenging during natural disasters. For one such account of challenges to the civilian medical system after Hurricane Katrina, refer to S. Fink, *Five Days at Memorial: Life and Death in a Storm-Ravaged Hospital*, New York: Broadway Books, 2013.

[25] A. Narayanan, D. Knopman, J. D. Powers, B. Boling, B. M. Miller, P. Mills, K. Van Abel, K. Anania, B. Cignarella, and C. P. Jackson, *Air Force Installation Energy Assurance: An Assessment Framework*, Santa Monica, Calif.: RAND Corporation, RR-2066-AF, 2017.

additional units can provide redundancy in access, which is a key resiliency consideration (as discussed in Chapter Two). However, resiliency in access to electrical power here is predicated on parallel access to another energy resource—namely, diesel fuel. Where this commodity may be more readily available, generators can perform reliably for prolonged periods.

In reviewing the role of additional energy resiliency, planners should also think beyond the initial cost of procurement of generator systems. To account for longer-term costs, it is important to think through their total cost of ownership, factoring in costs for asset maintenance and storage. Moreover, with the deployment of medical capability forward, it is essential to consider transportation requirements for these assets. Proper planning here will ensure timely access to the generators as expeditionary MTFs are established at forward operating locations.[26]

There may also be valuable lessons learned from the operation of other supply chains, especially in commercial sectors where cold chain management requirements apply. These supply chains include those for produce, frozen foods, and potency-dated items like pharmaceuticals and vaccines. Through an exploration of best practices in other large-scale, multicommodity cold chains, it may be possible to find valuable analogues for sustaining energy resiliency.

Communication Resiliency

Another key aspect of operational continuity within the blood supply chain is the assurance of access to command, control, and communications (C3). For example, in the provision of blood to forward operating areas, downrange MTFs typically funnel requests for blood through their theater's lead Joint blood program officer. That officer then directs an integrated list of requests from across the theater to the ASWBPL supporting him or her. With access to this C3 network, MTFs across the theater can rely on steady access to blood.

However, a communications-degraded environment may eventuate in the wake of a natural disaster or during large-scale combat operations. Under these circumstances, forward MTFs may need to operate with limited access to C3. It may therefore be important to train staff in mechanisms to send requests for blood through alternative means or channels, such as over infrequent burst transmissions or other low-bandwidth communication modes.

From the supply side, ASWBPLs may benefit from the development of alternative demand-projection algorithms, estimating downrange blood needs based on historical

---

[26] Access to support materiel such as generators can be challenging in the event it must be transported from the continental United States to areas far forward. However, a robust network of prepositioning sites can expedite global access to a variety of classes of materiel, deploying rapidly and cost-effectively to desired points of end use. For more, refer to R. McGarvey, R. S. Tripp, R. Rue, T. Lang, J. Sollinger, W. A. Conner, and L. Luangeskorn, *Global Combat Support Basing: Robust Prepositioning Strategies for Air Force War Reserve Materiel*, Santa Monica, Calif.: RAND Corporation, MG-902-AF, 2010.

or simulated demand assessments. Under contingency conditions with degraded C3, it may even be desirable to take a risk-averse approach of demand overestimation. In this case, the ASWBPL might choose to err on the side of caution, potentially sending too much blood and running the risk of high levels of wastage. However, this approach could serve, in effect, as an insurance policy, offering a greater chance of an adequate supply capable of satisfying surge blood demands.

Risk Avoidance

The foregoing discussion on the potential value in sending too much blood during contingency operations helps to pave the way toward a broader examination of another resiliency consideration: risk. In the scenario outlined earlier, we highlighted an inherent tension in the steady-state operation not only of the blood supply chain, but also of broader medical support. During day-to-day operations, the presumption is that the standard for patient care sets a boundary for system performance—namely, that high-quality care is the *sine qua non*. With a standard of care established as a constraint, administration of the supply chain can then focus on where system efficiencies can be improved, especially in an effort to enhance cost-effectiveness.

However, during contingency operations, the historical expectations observed during steady-state behavior must often be set aside. Consequently, to keep the standards for care high, the focus in contingency arguably may not be on efficiency (such as cost savings that can be garnered by just-in-time delivery of blood) but instead on the availability of blood for the patient (including by potentially sending too much blood to MTFs as an insurance policy against failure to meet transfusion demands). This kind of risk avoidance during contingency operations can help inform resiliency measures in other respects as well, such as mechanisms to limit the risk in using a partner nation's blood supply.

Making Partner Nation Blood Supplies Safer

As mentioned earlier, working with partner nations to secure access to blood outside the normal channels from the United States can introduce elements of risk. This is more likely in lower-income nations, where a significant element of risk is the potential for pathogen-contaminated blood in the partner's supply. Depending on the prevalence of pathogenic vectors in the region, local blood supplies could be contaminated by agents such as Zika, HBV, or HIV, driving a medical provider to weigh the benefit of transfusion services for a patient against the potential risk of disease transmission.

Technological innovations may be able to help limit this risk. Through the introduction of an oxidative agent, such as methylene blue or riboflavin (a compound in the vitamin B family), and subsequently subjecting the treated unit to ultraviolet light, a wide range of pathogens can be irreversibly inactivated.[27] These processes are especially

---

[27] For more on the underlying processes, refer to J. M. Mundt, L. Rouse, J. Van den Bossche, and R. P. Goodrich, "Chemical and Biological Mechanisms of Pathogen Reduction Technologies," *Photochemistry and Photobiology,*

effective at degrading pathogens such as malaria and HBV, but they tend to see more limited effect against more resilient vectors such as hepatitis A and bacterial spores. While FDA standards in the United States dictate the more careful screening of donors and donated blood over inactivation approaches, pathogen inactivation protocols are becoming more common internationally.[28] Consequently, one mitigation strategy to limit the risk of transfusion-transmitted infection is to support partner nations in their acquisition and operation of these technologies.

A separate dimension of risk is also possible with partner nations—the risk of denied access. In time of national crisis or contingency, the partner may need to limit availability of blood for U.S. service members. This may be especially likely if that blood would be needed to support casualties among its own military forces and citizens. This could prove a more daunting element to mitigate and manage in the overall calculus of risk.

Limiting the Risk of Adverse Transfusion Reactions

As mentioned earlier in this report, another risk factor is present even in the transfusion of a pathogen-free whole blood. Here, if a unit of donated blood is not carefully typed and cross-matched with a transfusion patient's own blood, there is a chance of an acute adverse transfusion reaction, such as hemolysis. In such a situation, the patient's own blood has antibodies that react with antigens in the donated blood. This is effectively an immune response in the patient against the donor blood, resulting in the rupture, or lysis, of the donated red cells. Though rare, this can occur even when universal donor product (type O) is used.[29]

One mitigation against the risk of antigen-related reaction may be drawn from the U.S. military's experience in prior conflicts, including the Vietnam War. During these operations, whole blood therapy was more common, with a general reliance on type O. Type O donors can be prescreened to determine the levels of antigens in their blood. Here, a donor can be evaluated on the concentration (or titer) of compounds such as anti-A and anti-B, agents that can increase the risk of adverse transfusion reactions in non-O recipients. By identifying those with this low-titer O whole blood (LTOWB), these donors can be recruited to become regular contributors to the blood supply chain. It is important to note that LTOWB is FWB, and as such it can be more challenging to manage at operating locations forward due to its 21-day shelf-life (recall

---

Vol. 90, No. 5, 2014, pp. 957–964.

[28] To date, higher-income countries have been the partners more likely to leverage pathogen-reduction technology. One such partner nation is Poland, which in recent years has introduced pathogen-inactivation protocols for risk abatement in its plasma supply. See M. Agapova, E. Lachert, E. Brojer, M. Letowska, P. Grabarczyk, and B. Custer, "Introducing Pathogen Reduction Technology in Poland: A Cost Utility Analysis," *Transfusion Medicine and Hemotherapy*, Vol. 42, No. 3, 2015, pp. 158–165.

[29] For more on the wide array of possible negative transfusion-related outcomes, readers should refer to Harmening, 2012.

the 42-day expectation for PRBC). Thus, the military's blood supply chain may need to be more agile, should its reliance on low-titer blood increase.

Conclusions

In this chapter, we explored a portfolio of mitigation options with promise for improving blood supply chain operations, starting from the MTF and ranging downstream to the point of injury. In this portfolio, some approaches employ lessons learned from prior decades, such as approaches for freeze drying plasma and refrigerating platelets. Other mitigations, such as using TXA to limit blood loss, buddy transfusion at point of injury, and parallelization of deglycerolization operations, offer recognized benefits but may not yet have entered mainstream use. Still other techniques in the research and development pipeline may become available in the near-to-mid term, including technologies to accelerate the deglycerolization process or to limit blood loss due to truncal injuries. Other evolving technologies with the potential to transform blood supply chain operations may require significant time to reach broader application, such as synthetic oxygen carriers to substitute for PRBC and bioelectrical stimulation techniques to limit blood loss.

We also noted a few more important elements of supply chain operation, including access to energy and communications. However, during contingencies such as natural disasters or large-scale combat, access to these resources may be degraded. This suggests the potential value in leveraging alternatives, such as redundancy in diesel generators and training to use low-bandwidth communication modes. We also examined how risks might be managed, including using technologies such as pathogen inactivation to limit the risk of transfusion-related infection from partner-nation blood supplies and the potential to leverage LTOWB as a mitigation against adverse transfusion reaction.

Thus far in this analysis, we have discussed a far-ranging array of capabilities for adding resiliency to blood support operations. However, the approaches and technologies were covered in the context of the qualitative supply chain framework presented earlier. In the next chapter, we will consider how to evaluate the relative merits of resiliency measures more quantitatively.

CHAPTER FIVE

Assessing the Performance of Blood Supply Chain Mitigations

We have examined a range of mitigations as they explicitly influence operations within the blood supply chain, including collection, processing, and transportation. Through this lens, this exploration has offered an assessment of how these individual strategies and capabilities can offer resiliency. In this chapter, we will think more analytically about mitigation strategies, especially how individual mitigations can offer improved blood supply chain performance. We will then examine how individual and combined mitigations can be compared to assess their relative performance.

Assessing the Resiliency Dimensions of Mitigations

As we originally explored in Chapter Two, mitigations in the blood supply chain can be useful in their ability to ensure more robust performance in the face of system stressors like a sudden surge in the demand for blood. However, individual resiliency measures may not be effective for robust support against all stressors. In thinking through how mitigations can strengthen the supply chain, resiliency may be seen within three dimensions: fractionation, composition, and functional substitution. As discussed earlier, *fractionation* allows for the scaling of a current capability; *composition* accounts for the combination of capabilities that may not occur commonly; and *substitution* represents a capability used as an alternate for one that is more frequently used.

Each resiliency dimension offers capabilities that may provide strengths in different circumstances. For example, satisfaction of a demand surge may benefit from fractionation, where existing operations can upscale quickly to meet the demand. Yet scaling up an existing fleet of cargo aircraft to deliver blood to a region where airfield access has been degraded will likely prove ineffective. However, in such a circumstance, leveraging the substitution of UAVs to deliver blood may become a more effective mitigation. With these examples in mind, we can examine the wide range of mitigation approaches explored earlier in this report through the resiliency taxonomy shown in Table 5.1.

Table 5.1 depicts how the mitigation approaches we explored in Chapters Three and Four span the three resiliency dimensions. Many, including the WBB, offer scaled

Table 5.1
Dimensions of Resiliency for Select Blood Supply Chain Mitigations

	Fractionation	Composition	Substitution
Resupply			
Airdrop			x
UAV			x
Production and collection			
WBB	x		
Epoetin alfa		x	
Partner nation supply	x		
Stem-cell reactors	x		
Buddy transfusion	x		
Processing and handling			
Faster deglycerolization	x		
Storage augmentation*	x		
Shelf-life extension			
FDP			x
Cold stored platelets			x
Synthetic oxygen carriers			x
Demand reduction			
TXA		x	
Wound stasis		x	
REBOA		x	
Bioelectrical stimulus		x	
Risk management			
Additional generators	x		
Low-bandwidth comms			x
Demand overestimation	x		
Pathogen reduction		x	
LTOWB			x

* While expanding the capacity for blood storage at an MTF was not a mitigation explicitly covered in Chapter Four, it will be useful to consider its value here. Refrigerators for blood typically cost several thousand dollars, and a larger refrigerator can hold about 300 units of blood. Storage augmentation must be considered carefully to ensure there is adequate available space and power at an MTF to support it.

access to blood, thus falling in the fractionation domain. Others, such as REBOA, are intended to be used in conjunction with existing practices in the support of patients, and hence are composable mitigations. Several other approaches are newer or alternative platforms or technologies, such as UAV resupply of blood and FDP. These offer capabilities that current approaches do not afford, and they are consequently functional substitutes. This taxonomy can be informative in determining what class of mitigation may be suitable to add resiliency in the face of a stressor, but alone, it does not assist in the ultimate selection of an individual mitigation. To assist with that, we will next examine an approach for comparing the effect of mitigations.

Comparing the Value of Individual Mitigations

While a resiliency taxonomy can help to identify the role of mitigations, it will also be useful to supplement this assessment with an approach for evaluating individual mitigations. Here, it can be useful to employ two distinct metrics to evaluate the relative value of several mitigations. For example, in the assessment of cost-effectiveness, one might consider both the cost to introduce the mitigation and a measure of its performance, such as the amount of time the mitigation can fully support patient demands.

To that end, let us consider a notional example to set the stage for a comparative assessment. Assume that a small MTF supports 1,500 personnel in a remote, high-threat region. Blood storage is available in a small refrigerator that can hold 30 units, which is a capacity typical of MTFs supporting a deployed population of this size. Given the threat conditions, it is expected that the MTF will receive three trauma patients per day with an overall daily demand for 20 units of blood. The threat is sufficiently severe that traditional resupply by truck, helicopter, or fixed-wing aircraft is not expected to be able to access the region for 30 days.

In this vignette of a challenging scenario for medical support, the small amount of on-hand blood storage will satisfy blood demands for only a day and a half, a duration well short of the 30 days until traditional resupply channels are available. Let us evaluate how individual mitigations might improve the duration over which blood demands can be met while also considering some notional costs for their implementation. In this example assessment, we will consider four mitigations: augmenting the MTF's storage capacity and on-hand blood, providing limited resupply by UAV, activating a WBB, and using TXA. As presented earlier in Table 5.1, this suite of mitigations spans the three resiliency dimensions, and we wish to assess how they differ in their cost-effectiveness.[1]

---

[1]   In this assessment, we will explicitly treat only a notional cost of the hardware or capabilities offered here and not the cost of any additional blood that is provided.

- In augmenting storage, we consider an additional, fully stocked refrigerator at the MTF that will provide 300 more units of blood to on-hand stock. This additional supply extends the time horizon for full demand satisfaction to 16.5 days. The notional procurement cost for this refrigerator is $10,000.

- For UAV resupply, we assume that, through contract or host-nation support, up to three shipments per day of six units apiece can be provided to the MTF. The notional shipping cost is $100 per shipment. With this augmentation to the existing 30 units of on-hand storage, UAV resupply can thus permit full demand satisfaction for a total of 15 days, at a total cost of $4,500.

- In activating a WBB to augment the small volume of on-hand stored blood, let us consider only steady-state donations, leveraging them from the fraction of the population that is type O. This percentage is typically 40 percent, and in steady state, donors would provide blood only once every 56 days. From the deployed population of 1,500, this yields a steady-state production of almost 11 units of blood each day. At this rate of supply from the WBB, full demand satisfaction is possible for almost three and one-quarter days. We will levy a cost of $50 per donated unit to reflect the price of additional on-hand access to collection bags, needles, and tubing. The total cost then comes to about $1,700.

- TXA will provide a mechanism to decrease the demand for blood, extending the duration over which the existing on-hand supply could satisfy needs. Let us assume that each patient receiving TXA needs 25 percent less blood. This effectively reduces the total daily demand to 15 units per day, so on-hand stock can now support two days of demand. Our notional cost for a dose of TXA is $100, so the total to support six trauma patients over those two days comes to $600.

We summarize these results in Figure 5.1.

With the capabilities and costs outlined, we see that each of the mitigation approaches offers an opportunity to extend the duration of full demand satisfaction. Furthermore, they each offer enhanced support at different price points. If only a single mitigation could be used and cost were no object, this analysis suggests the value of storage augmentation to promote maximum demand satisfaction. However, if budgets were slightly curtailed, UAV resupply offers a competitive capability at less than half the cost.[2]

---

[2]   It is worth pointing out once more that the capabilities and costs outlined here are notional, where we outline total costs relative to a scenario whose demands are identified *a priori*. In practice, a military planner would wish to account for uncertainty in demands, as well as the costs for potentially overplanning, such as procuring more blood-collection kits or storing more units of TXA than are eventually used. For this demonstration, the assumption of a known demand signal can still serve as a useful basis for comparing alternatives.

Figure 5.1
Cost-Effectiveness of Individual Mitigations in a Notional Example

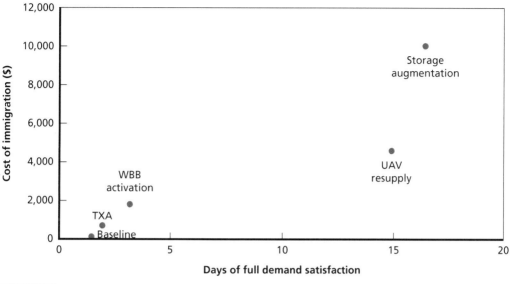

Comparing the Value of Mitigation Portfolios

The discussion of the previous section helps to highlight the benefit of an analytic comparison of cost-effectiveness between individual mitigations. However, as noted earlier, mitigations should be explored in concert with one another, where combinations may be able to offer synergies not apparent when mitigations are examined in isolation. For example, of the four mitigations presented in Figure 5.1, we would wish to evaluate how, say, activation of the WBB might perform if paired with the demand reduction offered by administration of TXA and to assess how that combination fares relative to each of its component mitigations. A comparison of composited mitigations based on those used in the earlier example appears in Figure 5.2.

Using the capabilities and analytic approach from the previous section, the figure displays how the mitigations perform in isolation and in combination, in terms of their cost and ability to support scenario demands. For example, in the case of a WBB paired with TXA administration, the combined mitigation approach provides a significant increase in demand support: seven days—more than twice as long as either constituent mitigation in isolation.

Moreover, several pairings are capable of satisfying demands over the full scenario duration of 30 days. Of these, the steady resupply offered by a WBB coupled with delivery from off-site by UAV provides full demand satisfaction at lowest cost—$10,500.

Figure 5.2
Cost-Effectiveness of Mitigations, Individually and in Combination, in a Notional Example

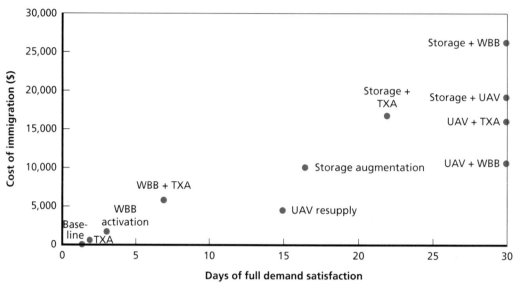

RAND *RR2482-5.2*

Note that this pairing does not include storage augmentation, which, as shown previously, was the individual capability with the longest-term support. Thus, for a small additional marginal cost over an additional refrigerator, UAV resupply in concert with the WBB can provide significantly greater coverage of blood demands. Moreover, this portfolio of mitigations offers capability to support blood demands far beyond the scenario's projected horizon, offering the potential for more enduring support if needed.[3]

It is also worth highlighting that the scenario inputs are key drivers in the composition of well-performing portfolios. Should alternate scenario parameters be considered (e.g., longer scenarios, greater daily demands, additional mitigation approaches), the composition of the most cost-effective portfolios might change. Furthermore, the assessments presented draw on the scenario's deterministic inputs. These factors could be recast in light of likely uncertainties, such as variability in the daily casualty load, blood demands, scenario duration, and rate of resupply. The explicit treatment of randomness or uncertainty in these parameters can lead to the development of more-nuanced resiliency portfolios. For example, investment recommendations could be established based on portfolios that are, say, 90 percent or more likely to fully satisfy scenario demands.

---

[3]   It is worth noting that more-diverse portfolios—those with three or all four of the mitigation approaches discussed here—are also able to satisfy demands across all 30 scenario days. However, each of these portfolios incurs a higher cost than the other mitigations presented in Figure 5.2.

Conclusions

Once mitigation strategies that might best add resiliency to the blood supply chain are identified, it is important to think through how those mitigations compare with one another and how they might fit together in a resiliency portfolio. In this chapter, we examined an approach to assess outcomes from introducing mitigations, focusing on a comparison of their cost-effectiveness in a notional scenario involving combat action in an austere operating environment. As demonstrated in that example, it can be helpful to assess how individual mitigations could be combined to leverage potential synergies. Through an assessment of a range of resiliency portfolios in terms of both their cost and capability to support blood demands, the approach demonstrated here can help to provide senior leaders and stakeholders an array of options to inform their ultimate decision in resiliency investments.

CHAPTER SIX

Summary and Recommendations

In this report, we have presented an overview of the Joint military community's operation of the blood supply chain. The medical community operates a number of entities across the military enterprise, offering blood collection, testing, processing, transportation, and storage services. Through careful administration of active and passive cold chain management, blood products can be shipped to MTFs around the world for safe transfusion into the patients who need them.

However, circumstances may emerge that could place stressors on the blood supply chain never before experienced. For example, a peer or near-peer adversary with significant missile capabilities could not only generate significant casualties during combat but degrade the freedom of movement of U.S. forces within the theater of operations. While they are unlikely, should such combat operations occur, the Joint blood supply chain may be hard-pressed to provide full support to combat casualties.

Consequently, we developed a framework for assessing how stressors might affect supply chain operations and how mitigations might come into play to add resiliency across the enterprise. Resiliency in enhancing access to blood supplies and their delivery to MTFs could be enabled by an array of approaches, some old and others still in research and development pipelines. Blood could be delivered by LAPE or UAV, where the choice of mode relates to the level of access to forward MTFs. Blood products could be secured with trusted partner nations, through WBBs, or potentially even grown in the lab using stem cell bioreactors.

To improve resiliency at the MTF and downstream toward the point of injury, mitigations followed a similar pattern of approaches, new and old. FDP and cold-stored platelets offer opportunities for products with longer shelf-lives. Other mitigations, such as TXA or REBOA to limit blood loss, buddy transfusion at point of injury, and parallelization of deglycerolization operations, offer recognized benefits but may not yet have entered mainstream use. Other evolving technologies may require significant time to reach broader application, such as synthetic oxygen carriers to substitute for PRBC and bioelectrical stimulation techniques to limit blood loss.

We also observed that some elements in the supply chain may not receive attention in resiliency conversations, including access to energy and communications. Given the typical consistency of energy and communications availability during day-to-day operations, it is easy to overlook the importance of energy and communications to operational continuity during natural disasters or large-scale combat. Furthermore, discussions on risk management are equally important. Implementation of technologies such as pathogen inactivation or product lines like LTOWB can offer significant opportunities in risk mitigation.

Overall, the intent of this analysis is to stimulate discussion in the Joint medical community to explore where resiliency measures may be needed in the overall blood supply chain. By examining mechanisms for resiliency across the blood supply chain, the Joint medical community can be better equipped to tailor a robust portfolio of resiliency investments. Such a portfolio would better ensure the availability and safety of blood under a wide array of system stressors and threat conditions.

Over the course of the analysis, several key themes emerged.

Systemwide modeling frameworks are essential to understanding. To frame a common basis for examining supply chain operations, it is critical to have a flexible, systemwide view. With a model that can account for and integrate a range of different supply chain operations, it is possible to assess resiliency measures that can support an individual medical treatment facility and those supporting a theaterwide network of medical treatment facilities.

Understand stressors that may challenge the supply chain. Whether undertaking an assessment of historical experiences of mass casualty events or participating in a tabletop exercise to explore possible future combat operations, a community of practitioners can posit scenarios both reasonable and extreme. When these scenarios are used in concert with a supply chain modeling framework, the effects of those stressors can then be examined to determine outcomes on the supply chain. The outcome of these stress tests will highlight supply chain processes in need of attention.

Identify gaps or brittleness in current capabilities. Understanding simply that an element is brittle is insufficient—knowing how it became a gap and identifying the circumstances under which it will fail are essential. For example, a supply stockout at a treatment facility forward might drive consideration for augmented storage there. However, if that stockout was more a failure of transportation to provide sufficient throughput of blood, an extra refrigerator will ultimately prove inadequate. With nuanced information in hand, it then becomes possible to think through the mitigation approaches appropriate to bridge the capability gap.

Explore how current capabilities, evolving technologies, and alternative concepts of operation can mitigate those gaps. Here, understanding the "why" from the previous point is most useful. For example, is there a functional substitute for the blood product that stocked out in the stress test? Is it possible to cost-effectively procure more testing or collection equipment that proved to be shortfalls? Could the limited capabilities of a forward operating unit be augmented by a small, agile capability from another service? A multidisciplinary and multiservice approach can help to better expose capabilities outside the scope of individual communities, especially in exploring the tripartite resiliency dimensions of functional substitution, alternative composition, and fractionation of capability.

Ensure that mitigations function at the scales needed. Some resiliency options, such as accelerating the capability to thaw and process frozen blood, can offer significant throughput capability for a short time to a local catchment area. However, if a broader network of treatment facilities requires longer-term support, leveraging options such as partner-nation blood support may be warranted.

Combined mitigations can offer strengths that individual solutions may not. It is essential to think through the broader dimensions of resiliency to determine where options may need to be linked. For example, partner-nation blood support can be coupled with pathogen-inactivation capabilities to ensure access to safer supplies. Similarly, combining the prophylactic use of tranexamic acid for forces on high-risk combat missions with reliable resupply of blood and medical supplies by UAV offers opportunities for longer-term support than either mitigation alone.

Ultimately, this process of supply chain stress assessment will yield a better roadmap toward enhanced resiliency in the blood supply chain. With adherence to that roadmap, the military's medical support network will be better prepared to provide quality care to its patients under a wider array of system stressors, contingency considerations, and threat conditions.

References

Ackerman, Evan, "U.S. Marines Testing Disposable Delivery Drones," *IEEE Spectrum*, April 17, 2017. As of December 18, 2017:
http://spectrum.ieee.org/automaton/robotics/drones/
marines-testing-disposable-gliding-delivery-drones

Agapova, M., E. Lachert, E. Brojer, M. Letowska, P. Grabarczyk, and B. Custer, "Introducing Pathogen Reduction Technology in Poland: A Cost Utility Analysis," *Transfusion Medicine and Hemotherapy*, Vol. 42, No. 3, 2015, pp. 158–165.

Alayash, A., "Blood Substitutes: Why Haven't We Been More Successful?" *Trends in Biotechnology*, Vol. 32, No. 4, April 2014, pp. 177–185.

American Red Cross, "Blood Components," online fact sheet, 2018. As of December 21, 2017:
https://www.redcrossblood.org/learn-about-blood/blood-components

Armed Services Blood Program, "Where to Give Blood," online fact sheet, undated. As of December 15, 2017:
http://www.militaryblood.dod.mil/Donors/where_to_give.aspx

———, "Joint Blood Program Handbook," Technical Manual 8-227-12, Washington, D.C., December 1, 2011.

Arsenal Medical, "Foam System for Acute Hemorrhage," webpage, undated. As of July 19, 2018:
https://arsenalmedical.com/products/resqfoam

ASBP—*See* Armed Services Blood Program.

Baker, Aryn, "The American Drones Saving Lives in Rwanda," *Time*, 2017. As of December 18, 2017:
http://time.com/rwanda-drones-zipline/

Beckett, A. B., J. Callum, L. T. da Luz, J. Schmid, C. Funk, E. Glassberg, and H. Tien, "Fresh Whole Blood Transfusion Capability for Special Operations Forces," *Canadian Journal of Surgery*, Vol. 58, No. 3, Suppl. 3, June 2015, pp. S153–S156.

Bouhassira, E. E., "Concise Review: Production of Cultured Red Blood Cells from Stem Cells," *Stem Cells Translational Medicine*, Vol. 1, No. 12, 2012, pp. 927–933.

Czura, C. J., A. Schultz, M. Kaipel, A. Khadem, J. M. Huston, V. A. Pavlov, H. Redl, and K. J. Tracey, "Vagus Nerve Stimulation Regulates Hemostasis in Swine," *Shock*, Vol. 33, No. 6, June 2010, pp. 608–613.

Dalesio, Emery, "U.S. Troops Get Freeze-Dried Plasma for Battlefield Bloodshed," Associated Press, November 30, 2017. As of December 19, 2017:
https://apnews.com/593dcb3902ed49a3b1adb97d824505aa

DARPA—*See* Defense Advanced Research Projects Agency.

Defense Advanced Research Projects Agency, "Advancing the Design and Modeling of Complex Systems," press release, Arlington, Va., November 20, 2015. As of December 18, 2017: https://www.darpa.mil/news-events/2015-11-20

Eastridge, B. J., R. L. Mabry, P. Seguin, J. Cantrell, T. Tops, P. Uribe, O. Mallett, T. Zubko, L. Oetjen-Gerdes, T. E. Rasmussen, F. K. Butler, R. S. Kotwal, J. B. Holcomb, C. Wade, H. Champion, M. Lawnick, L. Moores, and L. H. Blackbourne, "Death on the Battlefield (2001–2011): Implications for the Future of Combat Casualty Care," *Journal of Trauma and Acute Care Surgery*, Vol. 73, No. 6, 2012, pp. S431–S437.

Fink, S., *Five Days at Memorial: Life and Death in a Storm-Ravaged Hospital*, New York: Broadway Books, 2013.

Fisher, A. D., E. A. Miles, A. P. Cap, G. Strandenes, and S. F. Kane, "Tactical Damage Control Resuscitation," *Military Medicine*, Vol. 180, No. 8, 2015, p. 869.

Flynn, John C., Jr., *Essentials of Immunohematology*, Philadelphia, Pa.: W. B. Saunders Company, 1998.

Fritz, J. R., and J. M. Huston, "The Neural Tourniquet," *Bioelectronic Medicine*, Vol. 1, 2014, pp. 25–29.

Getz, T. M., R. K. Montgomery, J. A. Bynum, J. K. Aden, H. F. Pidcoke, and A. P. Cap, "Storage of Platelets at 4°C in Platelet Additive Solutions Prevents Aggregate Formation and Preserves Platelet Functional Responses," *Transfusion*, Vol. 56, No. 6, 2016, pp. 1320–1328.

Harmening, Denise M., *Modern Blood Banking and Transfusion Practices*, Philadelphia, Pa.: F. A. Davis Company, 2012.

Headquarters, Departments of the Army and the Air Force, "Airdrop of Supplies and Equipment: Rigging Whole Blood," Field Manual 10-562, Technical Order 13C7-34-1, Washington, D.C., May 23, 1989.

Holcomb, J. B., B. C. Tilley, S. Baraniuk, E. E. Fox, C. E. Wade, J. M. Podbielski, D. J. del Junco, K. J. Brasel, E. M. Bulger, R. A. Callcut, M. J. Cohen, B. A. Cotton, T. C. Fabian, K. Inaba, J. D. Kerby, P. Muskat, S. O'Keeffe, S. Rizoli, B. R. Robinson, T. M. Scalea, M. A. Schrieber, D. M. Stein, J. A. Weinberg, J. L. Callum, J. R. Hess, N. Matijevic, C. N. Miller, J. F. Pittet, D. B. Hoyt, G. D. Pearson, B. Leroux, G. van Belle, and the PROPPR Study Group, "Transfusion of Plasma, Platelets, and Red Blood Cells in a 1:1:1 Vs. a 1:1:2 Ratio and Mortality in Patients with Severe Trauma," *Journal of the American Medical Association*, Vol. 313, No. 5, 2015, pp. 471–482.

Holley, A., D. C. Marks, L. Johnson, M. C. Reade, J. F. Badloe, and F. Noorman, "Frozen Blood Products: Clinically Effective and Potentially Ideal for Remote Australia," *Anaesthesia and Intensive Care*, Vol. 41, No. 1, January 2013, pp. 10–19.

Holmberg, Mark, "Richmond Ambulances to Carry Plasma—A First for the Nation," WTVR News, 2014. As of December 19, 2017: https://wtvr.com/2014/05/13/richmond-ambulances-to-carry-plasma-a-first-for-the-nation/

Johnson, Lacey, Shereen Tan, Ben Wood, April Davis, and Denese C. Marks, "Refrigeration and Cryopreservation of Platelets Differentially Affect Platelet Metabolism and Function: A Comparison with Conventional Platelet Storage Conditions," *Transfusion*, Vol. 56, No. 7, July 2016, pp. 1807–1818.

Kimcheng, Hok, "Current Situation of Cambodian National Blood Transfusion Center," presented at AABB Annual Meeting, San Diego, Calif., October 8, 2017.

Lusianti, R. E., J. D. Benson, J. P. Acker, and A. Z. Higgins, "Rapid Removal of Glycerol from Frozen-Thawed Red Blood Cells," *Biotechnology Progress*, Vol. 29, No. 3, 2013, pp. 609–620.

Lusianti, R. E., and A. Z. Higgins, "Continuous Removal of Glycerol from Frozen-Thawed Red Blood Cells in a Microfluidic Membrane Device," *Biomicrofluidics*, Vol. 8, No. 5, September 2014, pp. 54–124.

McGarvey, R., R. S. Tripp, R. Rue, T. Lang, J. Sollinger, W.A. Conner, and L. Luangeskorn, *Global Combat Support Basing: Robust Prepositioning Strategies for Air Force War Reserve Materiel*, Santa Monica, Calif.: RAND Corporation, MG-902-AF, 2010. As of July 19, 2018: https://www.rand.org/pubs/monographs/MG902.html

Mercuriali, F., A. Zanella, G. Barosi, G. Inghilleri, E. Biffi, A. Vinci, and M. T. Colotti, "Use of Erythropoietin to Increase the Volume of Autologous Blood Donated by Orthopedic Patients," *Transfusion*, Vol. 33, No. 1, January 1993, pp. 55–60.

Mulcahy, Andrew W., Kandice A. Kapinos, Brian Briscombe, Lori Uscher-Pines, Ritika Chaturvedi, Spencer R. Case, Jakub Hlavka, and Benjamin M. Miller, *Toward a Sustainable Blood Supply in the United States: An Analysis of the Current System and Alternatives for the Future*, Santa Monica, Calif.: RAND Corporation, RR-1575-DHHS, 2016. As of July 18, 2018: https://www.rand.org/pubs/research_reports/RR1575.html

Mundt, J. M., L. Rouse, J. Van den Bossche, and R. P. Goodrich, "Chemical and Biological Mechanisms of Pathogen Reduction Technologies," *Photochemistry and Photobiology*, Vol. 90, No. 5, 2014, pp. 957–964.

Napolitano, L. M., M. J. Cohen, B. A. Cotton, M. A. Schreiber, and E. E. Moore, "Tranexamic Acid in Trauma: How Should We Use It?" *Journal of Trauma and Acute Care Surgery*, Vol. 74, No. 6, 2013.

Narayanan, A., D. Knopman, J. D. Powers, B. Boling, B. M. Miller, P. Mills, K. Van Abel, K. Anania, B. Cignarella, and C. P. Jackson, *Air Force Installation Energy Assurance: An Assessment Framework*, Santa Monica, Calif.: RAND Corporation, RR-2066-AF, 2017. As of July 20, 2018: https://www.rand.org/pubs/research_reports/RR2066.html

Office of the Surgeon General, "Emergency War Surgery," Fourth Revision, U.S. Army, Falls Church, Va., 2013.

Otherlab, "Industrial Paper Airplanes for Autonomous Aerial Delivery," press release, San Francisco, Calif., January 12, 2017. As of December 18, 2017: https://otherlab.com/blog/post/industrial-paper-airplanes-for-autonomous-aerial-delivery

Pabinger, I., D. Fries, H. Schoechl, W. Streif, and W. Toller, "Tranexamic Acid for Treatment and Prophylaxis of Bleeding and Hyperfibrinolysis," *Wiener Klinische Wochenschrift*, Vol. 129, No. 9, 2017, pp. 303–316.

Perkins, J. G., A. P. Cap, P. C. Spinella, A. F. Shorr, A. C. Beekley, K. W. Grathwohl, F. J. Rentas, C. E. Wade, and J. B. Holcomb, "Comparison of Platelet Transfusion as Fresh Whole Blood Versus Apheresis Platelets for Massively Transfused Combat Trauma Patients," *Transfusion*, Vol. 51, No. 2, February 2011, pp. 242–252.

Quillen, Karen, "Blood Use After the Boston Marathon Bombing April 2013," presented at AABB Annual Meeting, San Diego, Calif., October 7, 2017.

Ramsey, G. "Blood Component Transfusions in Mass Casualty Events," *Vox Sanguinis*, Vol. 112, 2017, pp. 648–659.

Reynolds, P. S., M. J. Michael, E. D. Cochran, J. A. Wegelin, and B. D. Spiess, "Prehospital Use of Plasma in Traumatic Hemorrhage (the PUPTH Trial): Study Protocol for a Randomized Controlled Trial," *Trials*, Vol. 16, 2015, p. 321.

Roberts, I., H. Shakur, T. Coats, B. Hunt, E. Balogun, L. Barnetson, L. Cook, T. Kawahara, P. Perel, D. Prieto-Merino, M. Ramos, J. Cairns, and C. Guerriero, "The CRASH-2 Trial: A Randomised Controlled Trial and Economic Evaluation of the Effects of Tranexamic Acid on Death, Vascular Occlusive Events, and Transfusion Requirement in Bleeding Trauma Patients," *Health Technology Assessment*, Vol. 17, No. 10, March 2013, pp. 1–79.

Rottenstreich, M., I. Malka, E. Glassberg, O. Schwartz, and B. Tarif, "Pre-Hospital Intra-Osseous Freeze Dried Plasma Transfusion: A Case Report," *Disaster and Military Medicine*, Vol. 1, No. 8, 2015.

Rousseau, G. F., M.-C. Giarratana, and L. Douay, "Large-Scale Production of Red Blood Cells from Stem Cells: What Are the Technical Challenges Ahead?" *Biotechnology Journal*, Vol. 9, No. 1, 2014, pp. 28–38.

Saito, N., H. Matsumoto, T. Yagi, Y. Hara, K. Hayashida, T. Motomura, H. Iida, H. Yokota, and Y. Wagatsuma, "Evaluation of the Safety and Feasibility of Resuscitative Endovascular Balloon Occlusion of the Aorta," *Journal of Trauma and Acute Care Surgery*, Vol. 78, No. 5, May 2015, pp. 897–904.

Scott, M., D. Kucik, L. Goodnough, and T. Monk, "Blood Substitutes: Evolution and Future Applications," *Clinical Chemistry*, Vol. 43, No. 9, 1997, pp. 1724–1731.

Shinar, E., "Be Prepared: Blood Centre Preparedness Plan in Disasters," presented at AABB Annual Meeting, San Diago, Calif., October 7, 2017.

Simmons, Dan, "Rwanda Begins Zipline Commercial Drone Deliveries," BBC News, October 14, 2016. As of December 18, 2017:
http://www.bbc.com/news/technology-37646474

Smith, A. U., "Prevention of Haemolysis During Freezing and Thawing of Red Blood Cells," *The Lancet*, Vol. 2, December 30, 1950, p. 910.

Soares, J. M., "USAMMDA and Freeze-Dried Plasma: A Story of Success," press release, U.S. Army, September 9, 2016. As of December 19, 2017:
https://www.army.mil/article/174904/usammda_and_freeze_dried_plasma_a_story_of_success

Spinella, P. C., J. G. Perkins, J. G. Grathwohl, A. C. Beekley, and J. G. Holcomb, "Warm Fresh Whole Blood Is Independently Associated with Improved Survival for Patients with Combat-Related Traumatic Injuries," *Journal of Trauma*, Vol. 66, 2009, pp. S69–S76.

Strandenes, G., H. Skogrand, P. C. Spinella, T. Hervig, and E. B. Rein, "Donor Performance of Combat Readiness Skills of Special Forces Soldiers Are Maintained Immediately After Whole Blood Donation," *Transfusion*, Vol. 53, No. 3, March 2013, pp. 526–530.

Tiberghien, Pierre, "Mass Casualty Events: Blood Bank and Transfusion Service Perspective—the November 13th, 2015 Paris Attacks," presented at AABB Annual Meeting, San Diego, Calif., October 7, 2017.

U.S. Air Force, "Blood Support Operations," Air Force Tactics, Techniques, and Procedures 3-42.711, 2013.

U.S. Army Institute of Surgical Research, "Joint Theater Trauma System Clinical Practice Guideline: Fresh Whole Blood (FWB) Transfusion," October 24, 2012.

———, "Joint Theater Trauma System Clinical Practice Guideline: Prehospital Trauma Care in the Tactical Setting," November 24, 2014. As of July 19, 2018:
http://jts.amedd.army.mil/assets/docs/cpgs/JTS_Clinical_Practice_Guidelines_(CPGs)/Prehospital_Trauma_Care_Tactical_Setting_24_Nov_2014_ID02.pdf

U.S. Pacific Command, J07 Directorate, "USPACOM Blood Update," Honolulu, Hawaii, 2015.

Voorhees, Carla, "Armed Services Blood Program Supports Patient Care Worldwide," press release, U.S. Department of Defense, January 24, 2012. As of March 2, 2018:
http://www.militaryblood.dod.mil/viewcontent.aspx?con_id_pk=861

Williams, Lawrence, "Just in Time Blood Delivery," presented at AABB Annual Meeting, San Diego, Calif., October 7, 2017.

Wong, J., H. el-Beheiry, Y. R. Rampersaud, S. Lewis, H. Ahn, Y. De Silva, A. Abrishami, N. Baig, R. J. McBroom, and F. Chung, "Tranexamic Acid Reduces Perioperative Blood Loss in Adult Patients Having Spinal Fusion Surgery," Anesthesia and Analgesia, Vol. 107, No. 5, November 2008, pp. 1479–1486.

Woodson, Jonathan, "Policy on the Establishment of Comparability of Foreign Nation Blood Supplies to Food and Drug Administration Compliant Blood Products," Health Affairs Policy Memorandum 11-008, Office of the Assistant Secretary of Defense for Health Affairs, Washington, D.C., July 11, 2011.

World Health Organization, *Global Status Report on Blood Safety and Availability 2016*, Geneva, Switzerland, 2017.